Kind Words

"If the thought of walking into a room full of strangers fills you with horror but you know your business will fly if you can just get the word out, then this book is perfect for you.

This week my 13 year-old daughter wanted to start a new club but was reluctant to actually sign up. When I asked her what the problem was, she said that she didn't like walking into a room where she doesn't know anyone. 'You do it so easily, how do you know what to say to people?', she asked.

I explained that it was a lifetime of working at it, practising, starting small and getting bigger.

I wish I had read this book decades ago and I might have got here faster. It's full of genuine advice and practical steps to take to be able to walk confidently into a small networking meeting right up to standing stage and doing your pitch.

The wonderfulness of this book is that it is written by someone who has been through it all and totally understands how impossible it can feel to take that first step. If you follow the genuine and practical advice that

Lisa provides in this book you will get there much faster than I did and your business will fly."
Claire Gilliam, Copper Knobs

"I loved that you can hear Lisa's voice throughout. I was reading it in her voice!

The visualisation and story-telling elements were great, but the way she explains why this is important and the impact it will have is even better.

I really liked the way that Lisa set out immediate gains, especially the profile architect.

Her warmth comes through on the pages, but at the same time giving expertise advice. I liked the style and the way the content was set out too."
Hannah Clarke, Solutions Hypnotherapy Solihull

It was a pleasure to read and very helpful for me too."
Hannah Clarke, Solutions Hypnotherapy Solihull

"Only 10 pages in and had my first lightbulb moment!"
Caroline Sammon, The Pet Sitter Solihull and Rebarkable Dog Adventures

Be In Demand:
Proven step-by-step system
for female entrepreneurs
with introvert qualities to
become confident, in-
demand speakers so you
can double your income and
impact.
Without experiencing
paralysing stage fright

FROM PAVEMENT TO
PODIUM

Special thank you to my closest and oldest friends, Kim and Claire, for being my 'ride and dies' and always being there.
Never judging and always supporting
I am forever grateful xxx

Huge shout out to Jayne Taylor Taylor'd Crafts, Caroline Sammon The Pet Sitter Solihull, Claire Gilliam Copper Knobs, Helena Pearson Helena Claire Coaching and Marta Suchomska Thriving Women In Business, who trusted me from the beginning and helped me design Be In Demand. Each of you is a wonderful individual and so grateful for being in my world as friends xxx

Lisa Simcox
Be In Demand: Be In Demand:
Proven step-by-step system for female entrepreneurs
with introvert qualities to become confident, in-demand
speakers so you can double your income and impact
without experiencing paralysing stage fright

FROM PAVEMENT TO PODIUM

© 2024, Lisa Simcox
Self-published
http://beindemand.uk

Table of Contents

Introduction

If I ask you how you feel about being in a group or a networking event, how would you respond?

Could it be that you dread the prospect of having to talk to strangers? The thought of approaching someone, who just wants to hand you their business card, makes you shudder.

Sound familiar?

The whole process is extremely uncomfortable, awkward and something you want to avoid. Small talk is likely to make you feel uncomfortable and potentially sleazy.

Success as a person with introverted qualities means embracing who you are and finding those strategies that play to your strengths rather than doing your best to conform to expectations of those that seem happy speaking in front of a crowd (often with extroverted qualities).

Where you can absolutely smash marketing, sales and speaking by leveraging your empathy, listening skills and ability to build deep connections.

How do I know this? Because I have proven it is more than possible.

As a self-confessed person with introverted qualities, there are two things I'd suggest to you. Your warmth and personality mean you can do this effectively and the second one is you can be who you are.

Now I am guessing you are reading this because, like myself, you will never be the loudest in the room. But you know, or are curious to explore, how using your voice is great for your business growth.

Because being able to speak to a group, no matter how small, is a game changer for growth.

I do not make this claim lightly. It is why the title of this book is about doubling your growth. I have done this for each of the last two years. But you will never find me bragging about this. You will never see me on my yacht or sipping champagne on one. You will never see me showing you a luxury lifestyle.

Because that might not even be what you are looking to achieve. And it is a dream not the day-to-day reality for most of us.

Instead, I will show how you can use your voice to grow your business to whatever level you want to. Whether that is the cliché now of 'a 6 or 7 figure salary' or having freedom to work a couple of days a week or working around your kids so not during holiday etc. The list goes on and only you know what you are looking for.

I cannot guarantee what success looks like for you but what I can promise you is growth results if you take action.

And the reason I am focusing on 'not being the loudest in the room' is for those of us who would describe ourselves as introverts or have introverted qualities.

It is your time to shine (I know, yet another cliché, but it seems fitting here). Because after what the world went through in the early 2020s has resulted in us craving interaction. We want to be around others, feel the energy in the room, and make real connections.

Which is where you come in. Because the beauty is that you have superpowers of listening and empathy which I will explain is so important in leveraging being in person and securing business.

The old ways are becoming obsolete. Especially because another person can find everything about you simply by doing a search on their phone. By being in the room is much more about being prepared and interacting with your chosen people.

The traditional transactional approach is not going to be for you anyway as it's based on you being selfish. Speaking to as many people as you possibly can until you find somebody who might want to buy from you. Acting like the proverbial social butterfly because you need to do it as quickly as possible to find the one person you can use to get what you want.

Worst of all, everyone in the room knows that's what's happening. And they're willing to accept that way to do business. For me that's just a shallow and stereotypical sales tactic (and so outdated now).

It is just not your way of growing your business or building a supportive network.

Plus, because you are never going to be the loudest in the room, you'll have been talked at by numerous people. They may well leave thinking what a great morning. But have they really? Or have they just developed a load of new acquaintances?

A bit like playing roulette in a casino. Where you can put everything on red or on a colour. And fingers crossed, hope for the best. You might win, but you're more likely to lose. There's a reason for the phrase 'the house always wins'.

How great would it be instead to build real connections, where you recommend and buy from each other.

Sound a bit more like what you're after?

Then read on, as you will like this.

Do you see yourself as introverted?

14

Being labelled as an introvert make you resonate with that statement?

If you were to describe yourself as a business owner, did you use the word introverted?

Just some of the questions I asked when I started doing research before I even put pen to paper for this book. Because originally, I was going to write it for introverted female business owners.

But then I got to thinking, is that just a label and may not really describe how you feel?

Well, it turns out from research I did, around 50% would view themselves as introverted, but 50% wouldn't use that label.

Which was interesting because when I did a call out to speak to people, I asked specifically for introverted female business owners. So straight away it led me to even more questions in my mind. Because fundamentally this is about walking into rooms full of strangers and having the confidence to talk. And initially I am literally talking about the ability to chat, not to present or stand up in front of a group or speak on a stage.

It started to get really interesting when I began to delve into this. The next lot of questions included

- How do you feel about walking into rooms of strangers?

- How do you feel about having to do your pitch?

- How do you feel about talking to a group about your business?

Everyone I spoke to, without fail, didn't feel comfortable. Here, it didn't matter whether they viewed themselves as introverted or not, because they all felt fear.

Can you imagine the response once I started asking more in-depth questions?

- How do you feel about presenting in a group?

- How do you feel about running your own events?

- How do you feel about standing on somebody else's stage?

The level of fear and anxiety started to go through the roof. And I got comments like, ' nerves get the better of me', ' I worry about what other people think about me' and ' what if I sound stupid?'

The latter responses weren't a surprise because for the majority of the population, because the fear of standing up and talking in public is worse than the fear of death (for 75% in fact).

16

Having those conversations made me rethink my whole premise for this book. And I realized the purpose was quite simple, to help women like myself who are never going to be the loudest in the room.

Instead of introverts, I now talk about women who have introverted qualities. And if that is something you identify with, then this book is definitely for you. Because you're never going to be one of the loud, outspoken ones. You're never going to be shouty in your behaviour. You're never going to consciously talk over anybody else.

And in fact, I will show you that your ability to listen is a superpower. And you can be as effective, if not more than those that are the loudest. They will still try and take over. They will still try and take centre stage. And they will still be unaware that that behaviour doesn't resonate with a lot of us.

They will also still be successful. Because their approach will appeal to their audience, their target customer. And there is nothing wrong with that as (I hope this does not come as a surprise to you) not everyone will want to choose us. But for those you resonate with, well that is your tribe.

It means you can be even more successful. You can be quietly confident that you will absolutely be chosen by your target customer for being exactly who you are.

So I ask one more thing before you continue on. Please stop thinking of yourself as a quivering wreck or a shrinking violet. I say this because it is exactly how I used to feel. Where sometimes I wouldn't even walk into those rooms, let alone start talking.

And please don't get me wrong, I still feel nervous today walking into those same rooms. The difference is today I choose to be there because of the impact that I can make on the other women in that room who are like me. Just by sharing a few ideas about how they can stand out and create demand for what they do, they can take instant action that has an impact on their business.

I choose to be there because of the positive impact it has on my business. The ability to connect with other women in the room means I find new business friends, I find fabulous ladies to collaborate with and I find incredible women who want to work directly with me. The ability to benefit from those you know, like, trust is amazing. And yes, it is a marketing cliché, but by getting to know you, to like you and trust you, leads to business growth.

It is my why for writing this book. And part of my overall why I do what I do.

After being in a successful corporate career for over 25 years working with big brands, I am so grateful for the opportunities that I was given. I learned so much from working with such diverse brands from luxury department stores to global hotel chains to high street retailers to airlines through to car manufacturers, football clubs and charities.

I built up an amazing toolbox of proven processes, tools and techniques to both generate new customers and also sales, with customer service being queen. Imagine being able to deploy that when it came to growing my own successful small business.

Who knew all that would be my training ground for what I do today?

And I'm super grateful to all the incredible female entrepreneurs who trust me to help them grow their business. Which means I've added a further five years knowledge, experience and expertise into that toolbox. Now 30 years of knowledge, skills and experience to choose from in my extensive toolbox.

It is why I'm determined to help as many female business owners as I possibly can. It is the reason I champion female entrepreneurs because for far too long, too many of us have remained in the shadows. And I want you to not only step out into the spotlight, but be your own spotlight.

The ability to stand out for exactly who you are. And for that to be the reason why your customers choose you again and again.

Where you can be like me and have introverted qualities but be quietly confident that you can make the income and impact you deserve. And all without one cheesy, sleazy sales tactic.

Where you can go from awkward networker to networking powerhouse.

Where you can go from event scaredy cat to event queen.

Where you can go from shrinking violet to gloriously visible.

How does that sound?

And even though you may not be the loudest in the room. I want to show you how you can be the most successful.

- To growing in confidence to walk into that room, whereas previously you may have struggled

- To growing in confidence to share your message that you believe in and watch it, having a positive impact on any of your target customers in that room

- To growing in confidence to actively participate in discussions and in putting yourself forward to speak to the group about who you are and what you do

- To growing in confidence to develop your own events that you could invite your target customers too, who choose to be there because they want to be in your world

- To growing in confidence to be able to
  - Stand on another person's stage
  - Share your story and your offer
  - Engage your target customer so they which will be cross oceans to buy your offer

Now how does that sound?

But of course, you don't have to be able to do all 5.

This is about finding your level of comfort to be in person, in rooms with your target audience. My hope is that you can achieve the first 3. So walking into the room feels a little less daunting, being able to leverage the opportunity to do your pitch, so that it's something you want to do. And to be able to at least test out speaking in front of a group. Because who knows where that could lead?

And how fab would it be if you could then move on to having your own events. They don't need to be big, in fact, I choose to do intimate groups, because I want to be

21

able to talk to everybody in the room. And I want the same for them.

Then hopefully to give it a go to speak on another person's stage. Because you might find the result is amazing. Not just in terms of your confidence but your ability to grow your business even more.

To help you, I've spoken about the different kinds of opportunities that are available to you.

Initiation - which are those first tentative steps of walking into somebody else's group. It could be an informal group that they get together from time-to -time, through to a formal network

Momentum - the next step of developing and running your own events. These are great platforms to invite your target customers to as they can 'test' you out and learn more about you, what you do and the outcome for them

Mastery - the third stage (literally, pardon the pun). Your opportunity to stand on other people's stages, talk to their audience. You choose which stages based on those that have your target customer. These are a game changer

As I said, no pressure to do all 3 because this is about you being comfortable. However, it is also about stepping out of your comfort zone.

I know how easy it is to stay at home

I know because I've done it myself.

I know though that doesn't help your business.

But in the past my struggle of walking into rooms of strangers has stopped me. Sometimes even when I've actually paid to be there. But then on the morning, my level of anxiety has just been so high that I couldn't go.

It is something I've struggled with for a long time.

While sharing this, it makes me smile at how surprised anybody from my corporate career would be to hear that. Because a large part of my job was about walking to rooms of strangers through to speaking on stages in front of hundreds of people.

I used to be open about how anxious and nervous I was to do any of it but it was never accepted, certainly not by any of my bosses at any rate.

But I was forced to do it because it was part of my job. I just accepted that I had to do it. Even though I would feel sick to my stomach every single time. So I learned to put on an extrovert suit which enabled me to do it.

The equivalent of going to network meetings today is the pitches I was part of with the sales teams. To paint a picture, this could be in Leeds waiting to walk into a

23

major supermarket's meeting room, in London waiting to walk onto one of a major film company floors or in London waiting in very posh offices before meeting senior people from a major department store.

I think it was slightly easier as I had a part to play and was representing the business I work for. Vs today when I am my business and I am just me.

And it always made me smile when the feedback from speaking on a stage I got was really positive.

Yes, I could stand on those stages. Yes, I could give an engaging presentation. Yes, I could come across as a professional speaker. Yet under the surface of the extrovert suit, was that shy little 6 year old who used to sit at the bottom of the stairs crying because I was being forced to go to a birthday party.

I share more in the 'how to tell your story' chapter. I just wanted to mention it here to reinforce to you that I don't underestimate the level of anxiety you feel. But there is a reason you are reading this. There must be a part of you, even if it's a small part, that wants to be able to do this.

Maybe because you know it will be great for your business.

Maybe because you want to step out of your comfort zone.

Maybe because you'd like to build your confidence a little more.

Whatever your reasons, you are so, so very welcome here. I want to give you the option of knowing you can use these channels to grow your business.

The power to use your voice to grow your business is incredible. Your ability to be in front of others or standing in front of others and talk about who you are, what you do, why you do it, and to be able to convert people in that group to customers in the room.

Think about when you've been to an event and you feel that level of energy in the room. When you remember the person speaking, who captivated your attention, as soon as they opened their mouth. Remember how pleasantly surprised you were to be entertained, inspired and spurred on to take action.

No stuffy presentation slides filled with words. You're not sitting there the whole time trying to listen but also read what's on the screen. Instead, being captivated by the person speaking and not distracted by anything around them.

Those are magic moments when everyone goes quiet as they hang on to every word being said. They might even be furiously scribbling in their notebooks because this stuff is so amazing.

No one sits there scrolling on their phone.

How much would you love to be that person speaking?

Now, before your fears start creeping back in, just imagine how great that would feel. Knowing that the people in front of you are hanging on your every word and cannot wait to hear what you say next.

And you know what? You can so do this. Because even if you don't think you are a natural speaker, you can learn the formula able to captivate those people.

This book is all about showing you what's possible. Giving you the tools to support you in making this happen.

Please remember I write from the perspective of having introverted qualities myself. My natural state is not to speak in front of groups, no matter how small. I choose to do it because of the impact it has. Not just my business but the fabulous ladies I get to talk to. I am able to have a much bigger impact than being purely reliant on the ladies I am able to work directly with.

This also has a ripple effect. I want those female business owners to tell their friends. I want them to share what they've learned. I want them to inspire others.

I'm no longer wear my extrovert suit either. It served me well during my whole corporate career but it is now in the back of the wardrobe, collecting dust.

I still get nervous walking into rooms of strangers but I take a deep breath, and I walk in there as myself. Other ways to reduce my anxiety are also shared in here.

You have got this. Walk through the steps with me and if you take action, you will be amazed at the results that you can achieve.

Are you ready? Let's go.

Chapter 1: Pavement to Podium System

You are about to walk through a 9 step framework I have developed, taking you from struggling to walk into a room of strangers through to being able to stand on other people's stages (if you want to).

You can use as many or few of the steps as you want. This is about stepping out of your comfort zone in a controlled and thought through way. With the objective of growing your business by being in front of your target audience.

Taking one step at a time, to grow in confidence and by showing to yourself, you got this. You will be amazed at the impact you can have.

But it is still about doing what is best for you. If being able to speak in front of small groups is enough for now, stop at that point. Remember, I have been in your shoes and still are to an extent. I still struggle to walk into those rooms even now but I know I can do it and I choose to do it. As it is fantastically liberating to know you have a choice.

My hope is that you take each step because you are incredible and what you have to offer needs to be seen and heard.

As a start point, these are the 9 steps so you get an idea of what each one covers. Included is a Point A and a Point B. In essence, Point A is your start point (where you are likely to be today) and Point B is where you could be if you take the step.

1. Motivating Message

Define your goals and craft the core message you need to share with your audience without having to spend a load of money on hiring a copywriter

To go from

Point A: confused messaging that doesn't resonate with your audience and leads to zero sales to

Point B: compelling message that converts leads into prospects 10x faster)

2. Profile Architect

Create a powerful speaker profile that differentiates you from your competition and establishes you as the go-to-expert without feeling like an impostor

Point A: confused messaging that doesn't resonate with you audience and leads to zero sales to

Point B: compelling message that converts leads into prospects 10x faster

3. Platform Planner

Establish realistic speaking engagement goals and objectives without feeling overwhelmed

Point A: having a speaker profile that doesn't engage your audience and makes you seem like everyone else to

Point B: having a powerful profile that differentiates you from your competition and fills your calendar with qualified leads

4. Pitch Perfect

Craft compelling pitches that hosts can't turn down without feeling salesy

Point A: Pitches that spark little interest for hosts so you go on the no pile

Point B: Instantly grabbing the organiser and getting a huge 'yes' response so you can cherry pick the opportunities you want

5. Storytelling Sorcerer

Define your brand's unique selling proposition and compelling personal story without feeling misaligned

Point A: Telling your story that bores your audience and everyone is checking their phones

Point B: Crafting a compelling story that mesmerises your audience and they are hanging on your every word

6. Stage Presence Mastery

How to optimise your stage presence to turn more strangers into raving fans without experiencing paralysing stage fright

Point A: suffering with off the chart anxiety and stage fright, just atso the thought of speaking

Point B: Being confident and gloriously visible on every stage to increase your credibility without a flicker of fear

7. Connection Queen

How to leverage connections, conversation and chemistry to turn leads into paying prospects without manipulating or pressuring them

Point A: No real connections or booked calls and being too scared to reach out

Point B: Being a connection queen and filling your calendar with ease of speaking opportunities

8. Podium Principles

How to develop irresistible offers and monetise your message without undervaluing your expertise

Point A: Fear of failing to sell out a single event and getting silence when you try to fill them

Point B: consistently selling out events through proven processes and crushing your targets

9. Sold Out Success System

How to sell out your stages and others stages without feeling sleazy, cheesy or salesy

Point A: feeling invisible, as if you're talking to ghosts with no ears or wallets

Point B: Feeling invincible, having people whip out their credit cards begging to work with you

Chapter 2: Motivating Message

The ability to convert in a room just using your motivating message is a real skill. And not one to be entered into lightly. Your message gives you the ability to speak directly to the person who you want to buy from you. Without any direct selling or sleazy sales tactics.

How amazing does that sound? But where do you even start in crafting a motivating message? To craft your core message. to share with your audience, without having to spend a load of money on hiring an expensive copywriter.

This chapter is all about your motivating message but before you can do that, you need to develop your goals and be confident in knowing what business you want to grow.

Because it is all about your goals, what you want your business to look like and the pain points and desires of your customers underneath. This will enable you to define a message that resonates directly so they choose you to buy from.

I see a lot of business owners who no longer feel as passionate about their business, simply because it does not feel aligned any more. They get stuck as they at are no longer in line with the vision they had for their business. And end up going through the motions and doing stuff for the sake of doing stuff.

If you feel like this, then the next part is going to be your chance to review the change you want to make in the world. And even if you still feel in alignment, it is a great check point.

Because if you are in alignment with your goals and what you want to achieve, creating your message off the back of that, enables you to speak in a raw and real way to your potential customer. Especially if you feel you are in the churn of just doing and maybe that has been working but maybe it also hasn't. Maybe it was working but not now.

I see it happen regularly when women I work directly with, want to jump to the messaging and content or sales strategies, but fundamentally there's work to do at the beginning of the process. This will support making sure your business is sustainably growing in a way that feels good for you.

Your first action is to dream big. Think about if you had the time, the resources, the skills. What could your business look like? Doing it this way means you've got something to reach for. Instead of just having goals that are easily achievable, this will stretch you to want to achieve even more.

There are no standard templates for small business goals or must-haves for objectives. And I'm not going to cover the basics of do SMART objectives because you can do an online search for that and be inundated with information.

Ask yourself what you want to achieve with your business in the short, medium and long term. Do you want to grow and scale? Do you want to recruit a team? Do you want to have a multilayer business? Or maybe you want a boutique business like mine (where I do not want to grow a team).

Obviously, goals are not set in stone and need to be flexible because as your business grows, things will change. But it is important to define what kind of business do you want to be. How do you want to be perceived by your audience? What are your values and beliefs to make sure that your business is aligned with them? Do you want to be in the innovator and creator? Maybe a disruptor? All questions to help you define, what is your dream business?

Alongside setting goals for your business, you should also set goals for your marketing and sales strategies. How many customers do you want? Who do you want to buy from you? What kind of people do you want more of? What service or product offer would you like to sell more of? What level of sales and profit do you want to generate and profit?

Setting these expectations will help you in mapping out your marketing strategy and plan. Within that you would include how many people you want to get in front of, how many small groups to speak too, how many events you want to develop, how many of other people stages do you want to stand on?

Within this you can decide month on month what kind of activities do you want to undertake. How many small groups? How many events? How many other people stages?

By doing this, you will have decided what success looks like for you. Which may not be the overused success factor of being a six or seven figure business. It may be that you want to grow your business around your family. Or maybe you have a set income goal to enable you to gain the freedom you want. Or you may indeed want a six, seven or eight figure business.

Your success is unique to you. And by setting your goals, you know what is on the horizon for you.

And please don't let your goals be something you do once a year and then file away somewhere. To use a cliché, it should be a 'living document'. Things change over time, so you need the flexibility to be able to keep refining your goals and plan, to see what's happening.

Now you have decided on your goals and what you want your business to look like, the next step is to help you craft the core message, to share with your audience. Without needing to have the skill set of being a world class copywriter.

It is about treating your audience as if they are brand new friends where you want to engage, learn more about them and show them that you absolutely get them. To show them you are the best friend they want to have in their corner.

40

The three learning outcomes are

1. Clarify the overarching purpose behind you speaking to guide the development of your core message

2. How to captivate your audience as soon as they hear your message? So they drop everything that they're doing and focus specifically on you because you have caught their attention

3. Craft a compelling marketing message that turns total strangers into raving fans so you can convert your audience into people who want to buy from you before leaving that room

But why is all this so important? Because, and I almost don't want to share this with you, there are gazillions of people who say they can do what you can do. Where your target audience has a constant choice of who to buy from. So how can you differentiate yourself to be their first choice every single time?

You stand out and cut through all the noise. Where your competitors can only stand on the sidelines and be envious of your ability not only to actively engage with your audience. But also that they run up to you at the end wanting to buy from you.

How does that all sound?

But hang on a minute. Your brain is already going into overload on all the reasons why you don't want to do this. Even though you know that being in front of your target audience is a game changer for your business, you're holding yourself back. Maybe the following three struggles sound familiar.

1. Just the thought of being in front of a room of strangers gives you stage fright. Your instant reaction is to run away, even though you're not even in the room yet. Stage fright is real and a normal reaction to being in front of people that you don't know for the very first time

2. Thinking you need to hire an expensive, public relations experts to even start to consider and being in a room of your target customer

3. And probably the biggest one, feeling like an impostor. What gives you the right to stand in front of those people and say that you are an expert and have the credibility for them to be able to choose you just because of what you've said in the room?

But how about instead of those struggles, seeing it as an opportunity? Whether you are in front of a small group of people or a major audience. This is your positive chance not only just to elevate your business, but also to get real and tangible results.

Imagin being surrounded by people whipping out their credit card when you tell them what you do. To the point of them chasing you down so that they can purchase your offer. How great would that feel?

And you have the absolute ability to be able to do it just by being yourself. Because those people will buy you who you are, what you stand for, what you stand against. And your ability to provide an offer that they already want.

No need to go on a major educational road trip to give them 10 reasons why they should even consider what it is that you're talking about. To have to explain exactly why they need this in their lives. Because if you have to do that, you are on an uphill struggle of making water flow back upstream, which we both know is almost impossible.

Instead, knowing exactly what your target customer wants so you can craft your motivating message to speak directly to them. So that every time you use your message, it resonates with the people sitting in front of you.

But where do you even start?

How about before anything, you understand why you want to speak and how this aligns to your purpose. By clarifying your overarching purpose behind your speaking, whether to a small group when you introduce yourself, to speaking in a group through to ending up on stage (who knows where this could lead), this will guide the development of your core message.

A great start is what you want to achieve through using your voice. Are you looking to educate, inspire, motivate, entertain or provoke thought? By knowing your goal, makes crafting your motivating message much easier.

For example, if I am going to spend a morning with a group, the purpose for me is to entertain but also to show that what I share works, by giving them small, actionable wins in the room. To build trust instantly and convey that I have proven my approach and if they are ready to stand out, this is for them.

By having a purpose behind what you are doing, you will not have to look at a blank piece of paper again and wonder 'what do I say?'.

Instead, your focus will be on how to turn your audience into raving fans who cannot wait to buy from you. By now you know the importance of your message...

1. To grab attention, the ability to say what your audience wants to hear today
2. To keep their attention, explain the transformation you are offering to them today
3. To prompt your audience to self-select, identifying you are talking to them from the start
4. To sound different, break the traditional model of 'I help...'
5. To make a lasting impression so when they are ready to buy, you are their first choice (which could be on the day, in the room!!)

The most important step is to clarify what your mission or purpose is, enabling you to carve out your position, to make you stand out. This provides the foundation to develop a clear and compelling offer, that your audience wants to buy.

Note: do not worry about the structure of your message, it is more about the elements so they are crystal clear why you are the best choice for your target customer.

Before we get into the juicy bit, how about a few secs to consider mistakes to avoid in crafting your motivating message.

- Focusing on income only – instead of what drives your passion. If you purely focus on monetary reward, your business may not feel aligned to what you want to achieve in helping your customers. The balance between joy and income is a strong factor in sustainability and fulfilment. For example, if your business is built purely on income and what you focus on in isolation, it will be apparent when you speak

- Messaging not being compelling enough – using jargon or buzz words instead of simple language that is easy and instant to understand and based on what your audience is looking for today
- Making things complex – being clear when you are in front of a group is powerful, instead of wanting to look like the smartest in the room so they buy

from you. Instead, simply demonstrating that you can help them and provide what they want

Fundamentally, it is all about focusing on your target customer and what they want

- It is all about them – your customers don't care about you until they know how you can help them
- What do they want to hear today – what are their deep struggles or desires?
- How can you show them they should care – what is the outcome or benefit for them

Great, so now you have worked out what you want to do but how do you make sure you make the impact you want. How about asking yourself three key questions that will help you frame how to instantly grab your audience's attention.

Question 1 Who is my audience and what do they want to buy from me?

Simply knowing that your target audience are in the room is not enough. You need to know them as well as you do your best friend. Now you could use the traditional approach of developing an ideal client avatar, sometimes known as a dream client or perfect client. The process where you identify who they are, give them a name, what age, where they live, where they have a family, what their hobbies are, what they do as a living, what magazines that they read and so on.

46

There's nothing wrong with this approach and pick up any marketing textbook and it will absolutely take you through this process. In essence, it is marketing 101 to know exactly who you want to buy from you. Don't get me wrong. I am not disrespecting this approach. Because literally, it is in every marketing textbook you will ever pick up. And something that a lot of the self-proclaimed gurus and experts will absolutely teach you.

What I'm saying instead is, those elements are practical pieces of information, but they are often defined around a person who doesn't exist. You are making your best guess on who your target customer is.

How about instead focusing on making an emotional connection with those same target customers? Because fundamentally, the majority of us crave connection. And by harnessing that approach you automatically start standing out against your competitors, who will blend in, as they use the same approach so therefore saying the same things as everybody else does.

Whereas you have the opportunity to be the pink Flamingo amongst the flock of those grey pigeon's. Instantly seen and heard.

To have the impact you want because you connect on the basis of values and beliefs. Where the audience instantly warms to you as soon as you start speaking. And because you take the time to know them so well, as part of that process you will define exactly what it is that they want to buy.

Back to the key point of being able to offer your audience something that they already want. Your ability to convert your target audience into raving fans who cannot wait to buy from you. And this is only the first step, there are still two other fundamental questions to answer.

So where do you even start? Simple answer - research.

You have a number of options here from asking your audience directly, listening to your audience through to good old fashion desk research. Ah, the final one takes me back to hours spent researching, pouring over data from questionnaires to opinion polls. Imagine being surrounded with huge stacks of paper that you have to go through individually to find what you're looking for. Verses to day being able to do a quick online deep dive into your target customer today. It is so much easier today and you can find free resources online. How great is that?

First step is to choose a search engine. There are a number available and they provide the information freely. Use the search bar and putting in keywords that your target customer would use to search for what it is that you offer. Now this is not about the words that you would put in because your customer is likely to use different words.

For example, if you help people with anxiety, it's unlikely that they put the words 'help with anxiety' in the search

48

bar. Instead, they will use the symptoms they suffer from and not necessarily appreciate that it's all down to anxiety. Instead, they may search for things like feeling tense all the time as they know they're on edge but not sure how to deal with it or get help for it.

So not only will online research throw up the kind of information that they would be presented with, but you've also got two great opportunities to more deeply understand how you can help? On the most famous search engine, as you scroll down there's a section called People Also Ask which shows you what other questions those same people are asking which helps you more deeply start to understand them (well that is what it is called at the time of writing this. If the words have changed, it is the first heading with options to click on underneath). As a side note, these also make great first lines for any piece of content, blog titles, questions or even subjects for a live video.

It is also the gift that keeps giving because if you sscroll down even further, there's a section 'People Also Search for' which gives you even more valuable information on the other things that are affecting your target customer. (As above the words sometimes change but the info will be there).

Remember, this research is only as good as the information that you put in the search bar. What you might want to do before even undertaking this exercise is ask your target audience what is it they search for. Simple idea I know, but

49

can be super powerful in identifying the words and phrases that they use.

Taking this action has a double benefit, not only helping you to do your research, but also the ability to use those same words and phrases in your content so resonates on a deeper level with other target customers.

Data is great, but will never be as powerful as asking your target audience direct questions. Your ability to ask questions and then ask secondary questions will really get you to the core of what it is that your customers want. With your start point being, what is it that they struggle with today? But not just purely focusing on struggles, because they also have desires.

Now the textbooks and traditionalists will all tell you to focus only on pain points. i.e. struggles. And they have a valid point, because what keeps your target customer up at night, what is it that they worry about? There is a stronger driver for finding a solution for it. So for example, a person will get up in the middle of the night to take a painkiller because of the pain that they have, versus the same person getting up in the middle of the night and taking a vitamin tablet.

But desires are still important and maybe even more essential for you depending on what it is that you offer to your customers. For example, as a travel agent, you may market yourself as taking away all the stress of finding a location, booking a location and having the comfort that

50

you've made the right decision. So you focus on a pain point? The desire to get away to your dream location could be as powerful for this set of customers and including this as part of your message could be the difference between them choosing you rather than another travel agent (who also uses that pain point).

I would recommend using different methods of research to get a really true overall picture and to more deeply understand your customer and especially, what is it that they want today. Because this is a game changer for you and I will be a broken record on this point., Offering your target customer some of what they already want is much more likely to be successful, meaning that all important sale.

Question 2. What sets your business apart?

Option question one has already got you ahead of most of your competitors because now you absolutely are safe in the knowledge that what you are offering is what your target customer wants. But that is not enough, because there may be others who also have that powerful knowledge and they are already offering the same people what they want. In essence, you need to be able to differentiate yourself from those other businesses.

And being a small business means that you are already a step forward because you can be nimble in adapting and being flexible in terms of how you provide the offer that those people want. But you need to understand what sets your business apart so that you can stand out. This could be as simple as who you are, and your confidence in being your unapologetic self. To be the Raspberry and Basil ice cream versus all the others being the most uninteresting variety of vanilla, because vanilla is all about sounding the same as everybody else. Which I know is not you, because you wouldn't be reading this if you just wanted to blend in with everybody else.

Take some time out to really think what makes you different? If you're old school, grab a pencil and piece of paper, if not, start typing. It helps use these categories.

Why are you different?

How do you do things differently?

Why is your approach different?

How is your approach to customer service different?

How is the outcome for your customers different?

This is not an exhaustive list, instead a starter for 10. For example, if I was to do this exercise, three differences I can talk about are

I ONLY work in person so we get everything done together in the same room with no one left behind

I offer the ONLY free and regular marketing workshop for female business owners in my area

I am super proud to offer the ONLY fully in person programme dedicated to female entrepreneurs, based on impact connections and solutions

Each element enables me to stand out and forms part of my message which allows me to be successful in the room when I speak.

Question 3. How can I instantly connect with my target audience to convert them?

If you've answered the first two questions and done the homework you have already part answered this question. You now have the ability to use your target customers keywords and phrases to craft your message, which will enable you to connect when you speaking to them. To connect instantly because you are speaking directly to your target customer in a way that resonates with them.

Next is to craft your message and I have provided a Motivating Marketing Message framework to help you, enabling you to instantly attract your target customers attention. Giving you the ability to craft your core message that you need to share with your audience without having to spend a load of money on hiring a professional copywriter.

By using the framework, you can be like a Brand Photographer client of mine, who the first time she shared her message in a network meeting, signed one new client and got three leads.

It is what I use every day in my business, where I can be confident to introduce myself to any group and gain interest in how I can help.

Summary

By crafting your Motivating Message, you can go from
Point A: confused messaging that doesn't resonate with you audience and leads to zero sales to
Point B: compelling message that converts leads into prospects 10x faster

Chapter 3: Profile Architect

Whether you're looking to speak in front of a small local group or indeed have the ambitions to stand on a major stage, your profile can act as a catalyst to make this happen. And the amount of energy and effort you put into creating that profile should not be any different whether it's a small or a large audience, because these are your target customers that you want to get in front of.

Using your voice in front of an audience is as much about being memorable as it is about being engaging. And it is easier than you think as it is about just being you, with your quirks, experiences and passion. No need to think you have to put on a professional speaker suit – as now audiences are more likely to warm to someone who is themselves and embrace the things that make them unique.

It is about what makes you different and your values. What you say and how you say it is what will make your audience respond positively.

A speaker profile is a description of who you are as a speaker a. And the credentials of why you should be taken seriously speaking in front of an audience. So no matter what the size of the audience, the principles still apply to be able to showcase why anyone should listen to you and why what you do is so what they should care about.

With any speaker profile, make sure that you don't sound like a vanilla speaker. What I mean is those people that sound like everybody else and don't take a stand. Doing their best to please everyone, but what they don't realise is that in reality they're not reaching anyone because they don't have an opinion.

Strong opinions are entertaining. You have the ability to take a stand and explain why you hold those opinions, based on what you believe and value, but also based on facts. This includes your opportunity to stand for something as well as standing against something.

This chapter is all about the Profile Architect. I have designed it to help you create a powerful speaker profile that differentiates you from your competition and establishes you as the go to expert to increase your leads without you feeling like an impostor.

The three learning points are

1. How to identify your expertise and perspective that speaks directly to your audience. This extends from knowledge and, experience through to the core topics that you are passionate to share about and have a great deep expertise in

2. How to use your bio to make a strong first impression. This is your alternative to being in the room with the person reading your bio, so it needs to reflect what you would say when you introduce yourself. It needs to instantly grab the reader's attention so that they want to learn more about you because it's clear you have value to add to their audience

3. How to showcase your go to expert status by using a simple 1 sheet format which leads to the development of open doors opening to new speaking opportunities and partnerships. It is not necessary or recommended that you provide reams and reams of information. Instead, to be concise, clear, and comprehensive in focusing on your core messages that make you the best speaker for this opportunity

All great so far? But as you've already found in the motivating message section, you can hold yourself back before even getting started. What do I mean by that?

1. Feeling unworthy ais a go to expert can stop you in your tracks. Your own self-belief is super important here. As you are the expert in what you are passionate about so why would you question your own expertise? Most of us have limiting self-beliefs, one of which can be convincing ourselves that others are better than us at what we do. But in reality, you do know your stuff. And you are the go to expert because you're passionate about what you do, experienced in what you do and genuinely want to help

2. Worrying about appearing arrogant. The fear of tooting your own horn when other people may judge you for doing just that. Even if you have amazing self-belief, you could still hold yourself back from doing this, but actually if you don't toot your own horn, who is going to? You should be confident in what you do and what you know and be prepared to say 'I'm great at this because...'. It is not arrogant to be factual in the description of yourself and

what you're capable of, so get used to blowing your own trumpet, because this is bigger than you. This is about having a bigger impact on the audience you can serve

3. Striking the right tone to ensure audience engagement and connection. You need to showcase your expertise in a way that will resonate with the reader, to capture their imagination, convince them that you are a great choice for them as you are offering exactly what it is that they're looking for

So instead of limiting yourself and worrying about being judged, imagine instead that every time an event organiser read your profile, your calendar gets booked. Remember I'm talking about getting in front of small groups here as an initial step and then build your confidence over time to be comfortable, to speak on a physical stage, if that's something that you could consider.

This is not about you freaking out about standing on a physical stage, this is about taking small steps forward, to gently challenge you out of your comfort zone because using your voice and your warm personality can be a game changer for your business. And for your personal confidence and self-belief.

The first step is how you can immediately capture the reader's attention with your profile. This is where you define your expertise and unique perspective so that soon as they start to read, they can't put it down. Because you're able to demonstrate from the opening sentence that this is someone that they should take seriously. And this is the case whether they're a leader of a small group that you'd like to speak in front of through to a Booker at a major event, the same principles apply.

Your ability to stand out at this stage is absolutely crucial. Ok pen and paper at the ready (or keyboard), to reflect on these key areas: Your knowledge, experiences, skills and insights that differentiate you from others in your field. What makes you different come is the reason you are chosen over someone else.

Once you're confident you've captured those core elements. The next step is identifying the key themes or topics that you are most passionate about and have deep expertise in. The ideal is to have several of these that can be tailored to any specific circumstance.

For example, so my key themes include 3 ways to stand out so customers approach you to buy, five simple marketing techniques to generate sales this week, how to be an in-demand speaker so you can double your impact and income without experiencing paralysing stage fright. Each one is about growing your business but takes a different angle depending on the objectives of the audience.

Great news so far, you've identified what makes you stand out in your market and also the key subjects that you have the greatest depth of expertise in. Now you can take that information and craft a bio that is compelling, making you a clear and best choice.

Your professional bio should highlight your background, accomplishments and expertise. And include relevant details such as your education, professional experience, notable achievements and any awards or recognition. The length of bios varies and may be dictated by the person you're sending it to. For example, under 100 words or under 250. If this is not the case, short and concise is the best option. This is not about inundating the reader with lots of information, instead to provide clear facts on why you are the best choice.

So you almost ready to write the all-important one page summary, that provides your profile. But before you do that, there's one key step here that before you pitch anything. Make sure you've got all the relevant materials ready. These are a list of things you need so you'll be taken seriously and will highlight that you are a real expert in your industry. To show your level of credibility that makes a yes decision to use you really easy.

1. Evidence or sometimes called showreels. Photographs or videos that show you speaking to groups as evidence that you know what you're doing. These do not have to be professional images, particularly if you are looking to speak in a small group. It is to show you have done this before and are able to capture an audience because it shows you're able to do this. For speaking in larger groups and especially on stages, I would recommend the much

higher quality images, both for photos and videos, as it gives a feel for how you are on a stage and it can be a key reason for being selected, especially on professional stages

2. Testimonials can be the difference between a yes or a no not today thank you. It is a really important piece of proof that you are safe pair of hands to be chosen to do this. That you can engage an audience and capture their attention, so they want to actively participate and want to listen to what you have to say

3. Information sheet. Often referred to as a speaker one sheet where you develop a one-page document that summarises your speaker profile which I will expand on below. It is for leaders of a group you want to speak to and event organisers, to showcase your expertise, credibility and speaking topics. Think of it as your chance to make a memorable first impression and showcase why you're the perfect fit for their group or stage

It should include professional photo, brief bio, speaking topics, key accomplishments and contact information. A great piece of advice here is to make it visually appealing and easy to read. Remember this is on one page so it has a big job to do and the easier you can make it to see the key points of why you should be chosen, the better.

In summary
• Headshot
• Logo & Tagline

- Biography (250 words recommended)
- Tangible benefits for your audience
- Point of view/what you represent/speaking topics
- Contact information
- Testimonials
- Clients you've worked with and logos ideally to showcase they are a real business

To reiterate, the more you could include the better, but please keep it concise. Explain how your audience will benefit from this, include testimonials from important clients. How easy you are to work with and what added benefits you provide (for example, complimentary copy of a book you've written, free guide they can download or a great resource they can access).

What the people in the group or audience will gain from listening to you?

Lay out the immediate and lasting positive impacts of choosing you. Remember, quality is better than quantity here.

The core elements to include are
1. Introduction: begin with a catchy title which captures your speaking expertise (think about how you title content to make it compelling eg 3 Ways to..., The Ultimate Guide on... or a polarising statement such as 'Social Media is Yesterdays Has Been'). Then introduce yourself briefly with a bio and focus on the value you bring through your experience

2.   Credibility: summarise any markets or audiences you have worked with previously (for example, I would include local female business owners), highlight your key selling points and accomplishments. Be concise in providing information, for example, use bullet points, short sentences and bold key points. Your reader is busy so needs to see the salient points within nano seconds

3.   Subjects: include the areas you are passionate to talk about, providing short descriptions for each one so your reader can see, at a glance, what you could offer to their audience

4.   Testimonials: use reviews of previous groups you have spoken to (if available), the ones that showcase the impact and value you provide

5.   Contact Details: make it easy for the reader to make contact

Notes:
Photos: ideally a professional headshot and any photos of you speaking to groups
Design: use your brand colours and layout (there are lots of templates available online too)

Now you're ready to design your own speaker one sheet using all the information I've provided. And to help even further, you have access to the Profile Architect Blueprint, to make it easy to develop your own one pager.

Now you find your expertise and unique perspective. You have crafted a professional bio to be proud of. And created a speaker one sheet that is used by professional speakers.

You can now take those first initial steps of speaking in front of a small group. This is how I started so I know how you feel at this point. And it is why I chose a small local group of friendly female business owners. I knew this because I'd already become part of that group and got to know a number of the ladies in there.

And asking to speak in front of the group wasn't as scary as you might imagine and was the first step to where I am today of being confident in speaking on professional stages that I choose to stand on.

In summary - in developing your Profile Architect, you can go from
Point A: having a speaker profile that doesn't engage your audience and makes you seem like everyone else to
Point B: having a powerful profile that differentiates you from your competition and fills your calendar with qualified leads

Chapter 4: Platform Planner

The ability to get in front of your target audience and use your voice is a super powerful way not only to build your audience but also to find new customers. With the ability to convert in the room just from sharing your message, can make a dramatic difference to your ability to deliver consistent income. Add to that the ability to speak in front of your target audience, will increase the opportunity number of people coming up to you at the end to find out how they can work with you.

But in order to leverage this ability, you need to be crystal clear on what is it you want to achieve. What is the purpose of using your voice to grow your business?

The objective of Platform Planner is to help you to establish realistic speaking engagement goals and objectives. Without feeling overwhelmed, and to fill your calendar with qualified leads.

The three learning outcomes are

1. How to establish realistic goals and objectives for speaking that align with your business strategy. Defining the level of business you want to achieve by using your voice is critical. As you need to have a purpose behind every time you want to speak in front of your target audience, otherwise you could be spending a lot of time, with very little reward

2. How to create a strategic plan for pursuing speaking opportunities. Planning is crucial, from defining the

speaker topics that you want to deliver through to researching potential platforms and then defining your ultimate goals

3. How to measure progress and adapt based on results, feedback, and lessons learned. Because understanding how to leverage the smallest of stages where you are sharing a message in a group through to the potential of speaking on a major platform, will ensure you're using your valuable time effectively

The Platform Planner encompasses all of the different stages that you have potential to use. And these can be categorised into three elements, Promote, Procure and Purchase

Promote
Defined as building your own stage, ranging from small groups that you can develop through to putting on your own events. This is reliant on having your own audience to be able to invite to your event. But you also have the opportunity to promote into other groups to invite your target customer to join

Procure
Defined as using other people's groups and events, where you have the ability to talk to an established audience of your target customers. This can be done organically through being an active participant in the group or by contacting the group owner to offer your services

Purchase

Defined as making a payment for the privilege of being able to talk in front of an audience. This can range from being a headline sponsor at an event to being one of several sponsors through to paying for space in marketing material for the event, including the ability to put something in the goodie bag. If the event is substantial enough, there is often the opportunity to have a stall to promote your business, either within the room or outside

So when you consider those three areas, the potential opportunities can seem vast and potentially overwhelming. Which is why it's important to decide how big you want these channels to be as part of your overall marketing strategy.

Otherwise, you may run into struggles which will hold you back from even taking the simplest of action.

1. Worrying that no one will want to listen to you, let alone hire you to speak. As even those with the strongest self-belief can still hold themselves back through being afraid of rejection. It is why tol plan is so important so you can define the steps to go through to build up your confidence, starting with a small step of just sharing your message in a local network group through to wherever your ambition wants to take you

2. Overthinking that your competition is better than you. This is a false belief. If you buy into your audience, they choose to buy from you because of who you are, how you

do things and the outcome you offer for them. So how about the idea of reframing, where you know you're an ideal choice in front of your target audience

3. Doubting your ability to find the right stages with your target audience. This can be alleviated through deep research, where you identify the opportunities available to you so you can select the best options for your skill set

So instead of worrying that people might not be interested in you, or you're not good enough, or you're not finding the right stages, don't think of it another way. Imagine after speaking, your audience lines up at the back of the room, begging for a chance to buy from you. How great would that feel?

Starting to sound a bit more doable? Great, so how about considering 3 core actions to take in order to make sure you can effectively leverage your voice to grow your business.

But before you do any of that, it's worth considering what your goals are here. There are so many different types of stages, from small groups through to developing your own and then being on somebody else's stage. You only have to pick a few that are going to work for you and then take action to make them happen.

Do you want to speak at one event each month or is it 10 maybe?

72

This comes down to the type of business that you want and what your aspirations are for your lifestyle.

For example, if you want to build a big business, you may decide that you want to be on multiple stages every month and travel all over the world to do it. Which means you're going to be hosting a number of events and speaking on other people's stages frequently.

Consider
1. Where are you at with your business? Are you still building? Are you an actively growing and established business?

2. What kind of life do you want? Do you want to travel? Do you want to remain local? Do you want to be online? Do you want to work face to face?

3. What are your business goals? How many customers do you want to buy from youme? What level of sales do you want to generate? What is your income target each month?

These will all help you align your expectation targets for speaking.

In terms of frequency of using your voice, maybe consider it as of choice of Whisper, Conversation, and Roar.

1. Whisper - low frequency of events each month, selecting one or two to target

2. Conversation - the ability to impact more people each month, three as a start point

3. Roar - multiple events each month

It is worth considering the size of events that you choose to target.

For example, Initiation, to speaking in front of small groups of people vs Momentum, where you choose the size of audience you want to invite (likely to be medium in size 20-50) to Mastery, of speaking on other people's stages which are likely to have larger volumes of 50 plus.

It becomes a simple equation frequency multiplied by size

Whisper x Initiation = low numbers, low volume

Conversation x Momentum = medium numbers, medium volume

Roar x Momentum = high numbers, high volume

Of course, there are many more combinations using the six options.

For example, Roar x Initiation, means multiple groups and networks to attend. In this scenario, you would be investing a lot of time to get in front of a small number of people and likely low volume of sales.

74

In contrast to the other obvious choice of Whisper x Momentum where you would target one large stage each month with the ability to generate high sales (with a high-ticket offer).

The choice is about what feels comfortable for you. Because this will focus your action on what it is that you want to deliver, from selecting the volume of events and the size of events.

For example,
Offer value £500
Conversation x Momentum of 3 events x 50 target customers = 150 target customer

Conversion of 10% is 15 new clients each month, worth £7500

Of course, if you offer is £1000 it is £15,000 per month.

The next stage after choosing the target you are comfortable with is the elements to target the events you want to be part of.

A quick note: when choosing your target, think about stepping out of your comfort zone and not go for the easier option. Starting small, with the ambition to get in front of a bigger volume of your target audience, will help you grow your business more quickly.

The first element is defining your speaker topic. You've already started to do this through developing your Speaker One Sheet, by developing the specific topics you can speak about effectively. Now this is about sense checking what you've already developed to ensure you've chosen the most effective topics. This process also enables you to have a pick and mix option depending upon who the group is and what your purpose is of speaking in that group. So that you end up with an a la carte menu of options to choose from depending on the outcome you want.

Pen and paper time (or keyboard). List out all the specific topics or themes that you could speak about with authority. Then review the list, and put a star next to the most powerful topics, so these are the ones to select to build a compelling title for. Because just like any other marketing activity, the words you use need to instantly grab attention. For example, below is a starter for 10 also structures you can use

Unlocking the ultimate secrets of x

Step by step approach to x to achieve y in z time frame

How to achieve x in y time

The Future of x is (dead, now y is the way forward) (defined in these 3 elements)

Find the fastest way to do x by y

In essence, you want to be able to draw your audience in immediately because you're offering them something that they want to know about. And it demonstrates your authority and credibility within your industry.

But please make sure that these topics align with your expertise and the interests of your target audience. Remember, this is about engaging with potential target customers so they want to then go on to buy from you.

After defining the topics, you can talk on effectively, the next step is researching potential speaking platforms of events. The key question is, what types of groups do you want to get in front of? As you have three very different choices of promote, procure and purchase.

So the first step is identifying groups, events, workshops, conferences, seminars, industry events and other platforms where you can share your message and expertise. There are so many different options to get in front of your own audience as well as other people's audiences that you need to be clear on what you are comfortable with. And in reality, you only need to select a few that you're comfortable with and are going to work for you. Because these are the ones that you will use consistently to become more visible.

Starting small initially would be my recommendation to build up confidence. This can be as simple as initially attending a few local network groups initially, to practice sharing your message, because that can be a powerful tool to be able to convert people in the room. It also enables you to get feedback on how impactful your messages are so you can continue to refine, as you should constantly work on that message.

It will also build your confidence within that group because you will get to know individuals in the room. So when you take the next step of asking the group organiser if you can speak, you will have already got to know the audience, so can use that as part of your pitch. Also, speaking in front of them should feel less scary because they were already a warm audience for you, and you've given them a chance to get to know you initially. This will create a much more powerful impact for you of being able to you share your topic.

As your confidence builds, you can start to reach out to other organisers, for example people who run workshops, small events and retreats.

This will provide you with a fantastic platform to move on to different types of stages, and you will have the comfort of knowing you can do this.

Back to your list where you've identified all the opportunities that are available to you. Now what? Next step is to evaluate the relevance, audience reach, reputation and logistics of each opportunity in relation to your goals.

To do this, you need to set your goals. At this stage, I'm not going to talk to you about SMART goals because you may already be aware of them and if not, an online search will help you. Instead, I'm going to talk about defining clear and actual objectives that you can track and evaluate overtime. I want to make sure that you're making the best use of your time.

I say this with knowledge of talking to a lot of women who go to a lot of networks and speak in front of those groups but either generate very little or don't generate any business at all. This comes under the category of 'fingers crossed' marketing, where you take action hoping to get a result. Instead to be intentional about your objectives of using your voice and then following up afterwards to further build the relationships that you already started.

I have already talked about your goals could including achieving a certain number of speaking engagements per year, reaching a specific audience size, receiving positive feedback from attendees, or generating leads for your business.

For example, you can have a daily goal of the action you take towards achieving the number of groups you want to speak in front of. If you make it non-negotiable and a daily. It becomes a core part of growing your business. And as this can be a fantastic income and impact generator. It's worth 20 minutes of your day. But it needs to be sustainable.

Each day you could message 5 stage owners through groups, events, etc, email two in- person event organisers, and then find two new platforms to contact. With the aim of one event per week to attend. Imagine by attending just one event per week, that's four events per month, where if you can convert one person each time, that's an extra four new clients a month.

The most crucial action is to plan, plan again and plan some more. And being purposeful about the groups you want to be in front of and how you want to use that stage is a massive step forward.

Maybe today you attend an occasional event or not at all. From tomorrow you could be leveraging your voice so you can confidently be with your target customers, having conversations about how you can help them.

But it all needs to come back to your goal. As if any use of your time, whatever the group is, does not fit with your plan or align with who you are, it will be a waste of your time. Much better that it is part of your plan so you know it is going to be a great use of your time and that of your audience too.

The research I covered earlier, starts now with a vengeance

1. Generate – find out where your target customer hangs out (local networks, events etc) and ensure you have

committed to talking about a topic that creates a result for them

2. Organise – create a document to capture all your findings, using a word doc, spreadsheet or google doc, to stay organised (whatever is in your comfort zone)

3. Categorise – now for the deep dive element, organise under specific headings, for example;, network, groups, events, speaking, sponsorship etc. For each one, identify the people or organisations to contact, and add information, links, special notes for yourself to enable you to review afterwards. For example, for a network you already attend, you could add notes on its potential. You can further make the data work hard by having three subject headings – Promote, Procure and Purchase – to divide opportunities between events you can put on vs other people's groups and events vs events where you can pay to speak or advertise your business

4. Action – allow yourself non distraction time (turn off all the pings and dings so you will not be tempted to check the message that has just popped through). Because this is time to take all the notes you have made into action steps

- Calendar dates – add any groups, networks, events etc you want to attend as part of your audience
- Group and event organisers – develop a list of 'prime' contacts, based initially on people you have met, know or you know someone who is

connected to them. In essence, a prospect list of contacts who you will use as part of the 'Pitch Perfect' step

- Connect – opt into any groups, emails, newsletters etc so you can stay informed of what is happening and when

5. Hot prospects – further refine your research, through your knowledge and experience. For example, you can ask your current and previous clients where they network, what events they attend, whose groups they belong to etc. Using your own database helps you factor in who to target

Special Notes:
Search engines provide a minefield of information to help you in defining opportunities, which you then cross reference with your goals. Worth mentioning that there is more than one search engine available as most will automatically go for the big one beginning with 'G'. But please also check out
Youtube and Pinterest as there is so much valuable data by searching on their platforms too.

As a starter, the key steps to make this easier are
1. Begin with a clear screen – no distractions of lots of tabs open

2. Use one word or phrase – eg Birmingham Business Network. Just one search will bring up a heap of results for you to work through, before moving onto the next word or phrase. Some results will be a multi option, for example,

Eventbrite or MeetUp, where you can click on each option on their websites

3. Open a new tab for each result — enabling you to research each one, before closing the tab and moving onto the next one. As part of the process, capture names and organisations, to add to your Procure section

Note: you will also have the option to click onto 'People Also Ask' and 'People Also Search For' to give you even more options to research

To help, here are some useful words and phrases you could use (it is not an exhaustive list and meant to get you started)
(Location) Business Network
(Industry, location) Business Network
(Target customer) Network
(Location) Business Event

Note: you can do the same exercise to find Facebook and Linkedin groups by searching the same words and phrases as above.

Also go old school in your research by looking at local newspapers, magazines and journals and free events locally advertised.

And the result, imagine you can be like one of my clients who was previously a Networking Queen, but had not generated the level of business that she wanted to. In contrast to now, where she's crystal clear on her message, her offer and her target customer so is now effectively using going to those same network groups to generate business.

Summary
Point A: having a speaker profile that doesn't engage your audience and makes you seem like everyone else to
Point B: having a powerful profile that differentiates you from your competition and fills your calendar with qualified leads

Chapter 5: Pitch Perfect

Preparation, preparation, preparation maybe an overused phrase, but it is a great way to illustrate how to be taken seriously when you're pitching for an opportunity to use your voice in front of your target audience. No matter how small the group, the amount of planning you put into preparing your pitch will pay dividends. Especially when you consider the number of people who are likely to be asking the same question, whether that is about speaking in a local network group, at an event or even on a professional stage.

How do you stand out so that your pitch is taken seriously and you're chosen? This is relevant whether you are promoting your own event, procuring the opportunity to speak in some in front of somebody else's group or looking to purchase an opportunity to use your voice in front of a larger audience of your target customers.

Pitch Perfect is a step-by-step approach to do just that. It will help you craft compelling pitches that your audience will walk over hot coals to get a ticket to, through to hosts not being able to turn you down. You can cherry pick the speaking slots that you want and all without having to resort to icky selling tactics.

Sound good so far?

You know the drill by now. The three learning outcomes are

1. How to effectively showcase your value as a speaker to make sure you are an easy decision. By doing your research beforehand, you can be more certain about having a positive outcome

2. How to grab your audience's or the event organiser's attention so you're chosen over others. With your ability to make this an easy decision because you've done your homework beforehand, so you're not only know what it is they want, but you also have the ability to demonstrate that you can deliver it

3. How to secure high profile events by turning organisers into your biggest fans. As your confidence grows, this will start to be a real possibility for you, even if it seems a bit scary at this stage

For the purposes of Pitch Perfect I'm going to cover both pitching to your existing audience to join you at the event as well as persuading a group leader or event organiser that you are their perfect choice.

Now I appreciate that your palms maybe slightly sweaty at this stage. But rest assured, I'm here to walk you through each step of the way. Because I know the prospect of using your voice in front of others can be a scary prospect. The following are the types of struggles you may well experience that can hold you back from doing any of this.

1. Struggling to find a way to tailor to your audience or hosts needs is a real thing. And we're bringing forward all

your insecurities about being judged by others even before they make any kind of commitment to you. But remember, this isn't just about generating income, it's also about making an impact so that you can help those who you've committed to serve

2. Worrying about really understanding what your audience or event host is looking for. But the more that you prepare and plan, means this starts to become a non-issue

3. Scared your pitch would not grab any attention and instead you'll be greeted by silence. But just like 2, the more you do your background research and plan, the more likely you are to have a positive outcome

Rather than thinking 'I can't do this because I'm scared, afraid, worried about not being good enough'. How about imagining the situation where you are able to secure platforms in front of your target audience who are there in abundance, so you can connect directly with them to build trust so they buy from you on the day

Ready to make this happen?

I will walk your through the 3 different types of groups and stages

Initiation – small groups or networks, containing your target customer

Momentum – developing your own events

Mastery – speaking on other people's stages

For pitching, I have not divided out Initiation because the principles of Mastery apply here. You will still likely have to 'pitch' yourself to speak in front of a group or network, where the framework of crafting your talks etc apply. The level of detail will be lower but the same process will apply (unless you verbally ask the organiser as you have an existing relationship and it is as simple as them saying yes).

Option 1: Promote

Before I talk about identifying other people's audiences that you want to get in front of, let's have a look at you promoting your own stage. What I'm talking about here is your own workshops or events where you invite your audience to join you for a specific activity. The reason for focusing on a specific subject or topic is to frame it as an opportunity for your audience to get something done with your help on the day. Talking specifically here about in-person events that can be anything from half a day to a couple of days and where in the majority of cases, it's you doing all the talking. There are, of course, opportunities to invite other people to speak, but you can choose topics that fit round a specific subject that will benefit your target audience.

MOMENTUM

Your ability to sell out the workshop or the event with your target customer, means using multiple marketing channels to fill it. Just putting a few posts on social media will not be enough to get the people that you want into the room. Consider instead a multi-layered approach where you get loud about what you were offering, as well as the offer itself.

There are a number of strategies you can deploy and I've included three for you to consider

1. Bundling - this is where you make buying a ticket irresistible by including bonuses. These can be access to special information or resources, as well as considering adding an offer that is already available. The more compelling it is will you can make it an easy decision. This is sometimes called value stacking and is a useful marketing tactic for any offer, not just limited to workshop or event.

You could add further incentives of anyone that buys a ticket to be able to invite a friend at a special discounted rate or to get access to even more resources. This is an effective way to get more of your target audience into the room with you

2. Multi targeted audiences - as well as your existing audience, you have the ability to promote to other

people's audiences to join your own event. Combining that with option 1 is, powerful as an offer

3. Multi-layered channels - the more marketing channels you select, the more likely you are to reach the number of the targeted audience you need to convert to buy a ticket to your event

Note: I have set out above ideas for attracting your audience to join a paid event, however, the same principles apply for a free workshop or event as well. I know this from my own experience of running a monthly free workshop since I started in business five years ago. The level of energy and commitment is the same whether you're feeling running a paid event or a free one. And I appreciate that may sound a little bit strange, particularly if you haven't run for events, but the objective is still to persuade your target audience to join you in a room whether they've paid for a ticket or not.

Option 2: Procure

MASTERY

Now onto other people's audiences, the first thing to do in selecting groups or events is utilise the research that you've already done as part of Platform Planner. You have a gold mine of information from which to select the opportunities that most resonate with you. Because this is about choosing opportunities that align with you and your business. It is not about randomly getting in front of an audience and keeping your fingers crossed that somebody will buy from you. Just in case there happens to be somebody in the audience who's your target customer.

This is about being uber selective in what you choose to do. And having that mindset, where you choose how you spend your time, will enable you to be laser focused on the opportunities that will bring you most joy as well as income and impact.

By choosing audiences you want to get in front of, you are more likely to be successful, because you're going to feel more passionate about it.

So once you've selected the groups or events that you want to target from Platform Planner, the next level of research happens. At the moment you have an overall picture of what it is, when it happens, how it works etc. This is about gathering information about the specific event. Including its theme, audience demographics, previous speakers, and goals. The more you can understand at this stage, the more likely you are to be successful.

Then you could have the second layer of understanding the group or event host. What's their mission, their values, and their priorities? This is essential information to tailor your pitch. You need to include these as part of your page to understood them and what it is that they want to achieve.

With your background information done, you can now move on to identifying you were tailored proposition to respond to what it is they're looking for.

Here you can use the information you developed as part of Profile Architect, look at what differentiates you from your competition and establishes you as a go- to expert. You can use this to clearly articulate what sets you apart as a speaker to be chosen. And to show why you're uniquely qualified to address their audience, in in the way that you will engage them to ensure it's memorable.

Remember, this is not just about your business, it is also about the group or event organiser as well. They are choosing to put you in front of their audience which is precious to them. So you have to show that you're a safe pair of hands that will add huge value.

To further support this, you should highlight your expertise, your experience, your achievements and any relevant credentials that will support your tailored pitch.

I have provided the Pitch Perfect framework to give you a guide on how to present this information. However, each pitch should be specifically tailored to that group or event. And you should never be tempted to copy and paste from another document because it means you won't have deeply thought about this specific opportunity.

Option 3: Purchase

Arguably the easiest of the three options to procure a stage, but the costliest. Many event organisers will provide you with opportunities to be able to buy your way in front of their audience. The highest cost being a headline sponsor where you are likely to be offered multiple marketing opportunities ahead of the event, on the day of the event as well as after. Or they may offer a number of sponsor slots, where you would still receive those multiple marketing opportunities. And as well as speaking, if they have panels, you could be invited onto those as well. It is worth checking whether you get access to attendees' data and are able to contact them after the event

All the way through to advertising your business in their marketing literature. This could be in the form of a brochure on the day, spots in their social media marketing, and insert into any marketing material, including goodie bags.

Depending on the size of the event, there could also be opportunities to have a stall or a table within the room or outside.

It's your decision whether you want to pay for opportunities. My one caveat here is balancing the level of investment with your expected outcome. So a crucial part of this is what you're able to sell on the day and how you would like to follow up with the audience post event.

So now all that's left to do is for you to complete your Pitch Perfect framework for each opportunity you decide to choose.

As a side note, a great insight into the other side of the fence is from the event I organised with myself and the addition of four other speakers. I was very selective in who those women were because I was putting them in front of my audience and wanted to ensure it was a great success. So their pitch was really important to ensure we were aligned in values and beliefs. Specifically, that it wasn't to be a sales fest but an opportunity to build deep connections on the day that they could then follow up with. On the day, they were able to offer free gifts but no direct selling. Because there are no icky sales tactics used with my audience and they were happy to reflect that.

The biggest advantage you can build is to forge relationships with those group or event organisers. What's the old cliché? Your network is your net worth. Which although it makes me cringe just to say it, is relevant in this case. Building relationships with those people is one of the best things you can do to get yourself selected. And that's whether to speak at a network meeting, participating in a workshop or speaking on their stage.

But how do you do that without becoming annoying? Really, it's the same that you do when building any connection, make friendly contact first, offer to provide any help that you can and genuinely get to know the person. These are potential fantastic business buddies and

96

great relationships for your businesses. So the more you invest in the early stages, the more likely it is to pay off.

You could choose the obvious route of sending an email, particularly if you're new to this person, but that's what everyone else will do. How about instead sending them a friendly voice note, complimenting them on what they do and maybe an offer of help.

Who knows where that developing relationship could lead? And when you do pitch to be in front of their group or audience, the worst they can say is 'not today'. And as the favourite salesperson I ever worked with said, 'it's just a no today. Tomorrow it could be a yes'.

Summary
Point A: Pitches that spark little interest for hosts so you go on the no pile
Point B: Instantly grabbing the organiser and getting a huge 'yes' response so you can cherry pick the opportunities you want

Chapter 6: Storytelling Sorcerer

Once upon a time is a story that we all know, and from a young age our brains are wired to love stories. The evidence is around us everywhere, especially in the movies that we watch as the majority are story based in theme. There's a start and middle and an end to take us through the ups and downs of emotions so we feel the story every step of the way.

Think back to when you were a child or when you've read a child a story. Wouldn't she When you get to the end? What's the question? The single word that's uttered and you know, you've got to go back to the beginning. Yes, you guessed it, the word is very simple but powerful. 'Again'. The repetition of the story over and over again never gets tired for small children. So what more proof do you want or need than the fact we are hardwired from being very young to love stories.

When I was young, which was a very long time ago now, there was a TV programme called Jackanory. The format of the show was a famous actor reading from children's books. And seated in a comfy armchair. The idea behind the show was to encourage an interest in reading. So It was all about stories and children would look forward to every episode.

Think about the success of the Hollywood film industry. We can't get enough of the stories they churn out week after week after week. And how many times have you watched the same film purely because you love the story?

Another case is the success of soap operas. Now, the term soap opera originated from radio dramas that were sponsored by soap manufacturers. Consider the world's longest running radio soap opera, The Archers, that first broadcast in 1950. The defining feature of soap operas is that it's an continuous story. At the end of each episode, there's a promise that the story will be continued in the next episode. Where the storylines running parallel intersect and then lead into future storylines. Individual episodes turn into their its own story, but are then linked to all of the other episodes which holds maintains our attention.

And if you're still not convinced, that our brains are hardwired to love stories. Think about millions of years ago when writing didn't even exist. Our ancestors would gather round the fire and tell each other's stories which included important learnings that could be carried on through generations. Even in caves, stories were told visually in pictures to explain every step of the story. So guess what? Our brains hear a story and say 'I need to listen to this'.

Imagine, then, how powerful telling stories is to show both the person you are pitching to the story to, and when you tell it in front of an audience, just how powerful and compelling it is.

The power of being a storyteller really is the difference between using speaking to grow your business or just spending time having a bit of a chat in front of a group. The storytellers are able to make the audience laugh and cry and even get a huge round of applause or even standing ovation at the end. In contrast, the people who might have amazing content, but where the audience are bored and sitting there scrolling through their phones or looking around the room, or even worse, leaving.

This is much more like putting on a show. Think of yourself as P T Barnum in The Greatest Showman where he captured the audience's imagination from the moment he stepped into the ring. What can we learn from that?

Immediately grab your audience's attention

Get your audience to like you straight away

Keep your audience riveted

Create wow and memorable moments

Get invited back again and again

A great five-point checklist to consider as you're writing. And to check against when you practicing.

Because your audience are also considering five things when they're listening to you:

Do I like the speaker?

Do I like what they're saying?

103

Does what they're saying matter to me.

What makes them credible to even be here?

Do they care about ME?

Many things reinforce how important connecting emotionally is. Because of that all-important trust factor and your ability to not only resonate with them but get a positive reaction out of them as well.

Storytelling Sorcerer is all about helping you define your personal story linked to your business, which will cover multiple elements from your origin story through to individual stories that have happened along the way. Because stories are proven to increase engagement.

Crafting your stories helps you make an emotional connection to your audience without it feeling misaligned because this is about you and you are your business.

Now are you sitting comfortably? Then I'll begin (if you do not recognise the phrase, it was used by an old TV programme called Listen With Mother). How could I resist using the line when this is all about creating your story?

The three learning outcomes for Storytelling Sorcerer are.

1. How to strengthen your brand identity so you stand out from your target customer. Stories are a powerful way to entertain and engage with your audience but as

importantly, to emotionally connect with them because it will resonate

2. How to use your personal story to connect on an emotional level. Just telling the story is not enough. It is about the way you share the details. Your reader will nod along because they have experienced something similar or it appeals to them

3. How choosing meaningful stories helps your audience become loyal followers. The word meaningful is very important as you select the stories that are most likely to connect

The first thing I want to share is that I appreciate that not everybody is a natural storyteller. It is not something we're taught in school. But how great would that be that rather than dry English lessons, we were taught how to construct a fantastic story. Imagine how we could all be international bestsellers if that was the case!

Instead, you might be feeling ill sick at the idea of sharing personal stories. So before I continue, I would like to share 3 tests that you can go through before sharing any story

1. Would you feel comfortable sharing the story with a close relative? It is the first step along the way because if the answer is no, then don't share

2. Would you feel comfortable if your story ended up as a headline in a newspaper? This might seem like an odd one,

but if you are sharing with your audience, is in the public domain. So in theory, it could get picked up by a journalist. In reality, this is unlikely but still a good test

3. The final one is how you feel about the thought of sharing your story in public. If you have a few butterflies, that can be a good thing because it's showing you you're stepping slightly out of your comfort zone. But if you feel sick to your stomach, don't do it

Bearing those in mind, you might still have a few more struggles to deal with.

1. The fear of judgment or backlash from sharing your story can be strong and stop you doing this. So the challenge is, why do you have those fears? And maybe considering the three tests above can help in this situation. And I always find using the phrase 'what's the worst that can happen?' he's a really useful one. Really, what is the risk of sharing? Especially when you consider the positive opportunity to really connect with your audience

2. Being worried about how to share your story in a genuine way. A couple of things here to consider. The first is to write your story in your words. What I mean by that is simply start writing and don't stop as this will make sure it sounds like you. And if easier, record yourself telling the story. Then by all means you can go back and edit it, check for any typos, etc but please do not check for grammar. Simply because we don't speak in a grammatically correct way. The second thing linked to don't stop writing is so that

106

it comes straight from the heart. First one, use the stopwatch on your phone and give yourself 2 minutes. You'll be amazed at how much you can write in those 120 seconds

3. Fretting about oversharing and losing your audience. If your story comes from a genuine place, your audience are likely to be compelled to read on and not get lost. And in terms of over sharing, refer back to the three tests in this chapter. If your story passes all three tests, that will hopefully reinforce to you that you are comfortable to share

So now imagine how fantastic it is to create a powerful emotional connection with your targeted audience so that they approach you to buy. And that is exactly what sharing stories can do for you.

Whether you are working on INITIATION, MOMEUMTUM OR MASTERY stages, the only difference is the level of stories you share. For INIATITION, you may share one or two stories as you time may be limited to 10-15 minutes vs in your own event. For MOMENTUM, you choose how much time you have. Finally, for MASTERY, it will be time dependant but even if it is 15 minutes, unlike INITIATION, you will tell many more stories as you have a bigger audience to engage.

Choosing a relevant and meaningful topic is the first step. I appreciate that might sound a bit vague but this is where the magic lies. Your ability to select a personal experience or anecdote that's relevant to the theme or message you want to convey, will deliver you positive results.

Consider experiences that have had significant impact on your life, shaped your beliefs or taught you valuable lessons.

For example, I share the story of how I decided to leave my successful career in the world of corporate. Especially when I explain the catalyst was being promoted to Managing Director, which was the day I decided to leave. Because it meant spending my work life in a series of three-hour committee meetings and taking me further and further away from what I was passionate about, developing my team and marketing. After my promotion, I'd stuck around for 12 months to ensure that my team was self-sufficient and I could leave with a clear conscience.

Apart from a select trusted few, I stayed silent about my overall plan, so the shock of people around me when I finally resigned was not surprised. I was leaving a safe, salaried position for the unknown. To me it was exciting and who knew I would find a new passion, with the most incredible women and get to make a real difference and impact on their lives.

Now I know the story resonates with a lot of women in my audience who, like me, had a previous corporate career. And one where they took the brave decision to grow their own business. The reasons behind them leaving may be different from mine but the overall story will still resonate.

Once you've decided on the story or stories you want to share, the next step is establishing a clear narrative arc. Wow, how fancy does that sound? Int's slightly easier to understand words, as I'm a big fan of simple, it is about structuring your story with a clear beginning, middle and end. A structure exactly like any good 'Once Upon a Time' story'.

Within the framework, the idea is to develop a roller coaster of emotions. So creating a story that builds tension, engages the audience's emotions and resolves in a satisfactory way ie positive outcome.

This is where you put on your script writer's hat. Where you introduce the setting, characters and context to establish the overall scene and draw your audience into your story.

You need to build tension or conflict to maintain your audience's attention. This is about bringing to life the actions, challenges, obstacles and dilemmas that you face during the experience. And finally, to reach a climax or turning point where the stakes are highest, followed by resolution or conclusion that provides both closure and insight.

For example, in my story above I could talk about some of the actions I took where I thought I might have been found out on my plan to leave. Especially when I started clearing out the big cupboards both in my office and outside because I was well known for squirreling papers away. But they're not looking at them again!! To the point where I struggled to close the cupboard doors. And every time I open them, papers would fall out on me. So to suddenly have a clear out was unusual and I was questioned about it by multiple people, laughing it off each time as a spring clean.

Or the challenge of, would I be brave enough at the end to resign? Yes, it was the plan, but would I be able to go through with it? Turns out it was an easy decision to go through with it in the end, when the thought of one more three-hour committee meeting filled me with dread. Penning the letter was a huge emotional release. And the conclusion was walking away which I have never regretted for one nanosecond.

Hopefully this helps illustrate how you can tell stories within stories too.

To make your stories come to life and be much more engaging for your audience, there are several techniques you can use to deepen the engagement and therefore connection. These are proven techniques that have been used again and again by speakers over time.

Storytelling techniques you can be used in a variety of ways, with the core objective being that your audience find your story unforgettable. Yes, the words you choose are important, but as important is the way that you make them feel. There are unlikely to remember numbers or statistics, but they will remember how they felt during and at the end of your story. That is when you know you've captured their attention, you've spoken to their hearts, and they are much more likely to want to choose you.

I've included some simple techniques below, but this is not an exhaustive list. Books and books and books have been written about storytelling techniques so what I've done is captured a few of the ones that I've used again and again and proven to work.

Action Focus - jumping into your story with immediate action brings the listener in because spending too much time on context not only wastes time, but actually loses your audience. So starting with the action means that you're talking about you or somebody else.

What kind of action are they taking? Are they walking? Are they jumping in? Are they hopping in on something? Stepping into somewhere? Reading something? So, for example, 'I remember this time the same time last year, I ran into the room only to find...'.

In essence, you start your story with momentum, so you're bringing your listeners or readers into the sort story straight away. Because they want to know 'What's going on? Where's this going? What's happening?'.

Dialogue
This is the use of two or more characters speaking. So for any story you were telling, to be able to capture a

conversation and relay that to your audience will bring them in closer. It helps you paint a picture that's more vivid. Enables your story to come to life because you are using real people to explain pivotal parts within your story. In essence, you are transporting your reader or listener into the world of your story. You want to paint a picture so they can see the scene in their heads, feel the emotions, and experience the story as if they were there and it was happening to them.

It is why wide dialogue can be so important. For example. Instead of saying 'my boss was very disappointed in me' say 'my boss bellowed in my ear, "you are a complete waste of time and effort, get out of here"'. Instead of saying 'my client got a new order' say 'Josie called me and said "Lisa, it is absolutely amazing. I've just got the best order through, which means that I have had my best month ever. Woohoo."'.

They're really small changes, but it can make a huge difference to story. And don't worry if you can't remember the exact words that were used in the conversation. Because that's the beauty of telling a story, that you have creative freedom to say what you thought was said in that particular moment. What kind of words would have been used?

Pacing
Using a difference in the speed of presenting your story. Both fast and slow means that your audience is always on the edge of their seats. Versus being monotone in your

112

delivery which can sound flat. Instead using changes of speed he's is more likely to capture interest. When you want to slow things down, use descriptive sentences. And when you want to speed it up, that's where you can use action scenes and particularly dialogue where people are speaking to each other. You can also use action elements to slow down specific moments when you want to build suspense that I'm about to come on to.

One method is using breathers where you explain what's going on. And these are great to use to balance the action elements of your story, which tend to be faster paced. Changing the order of events is also a well-known tactic where you can start your story in the middle of the action and then fill details in later. This works well if you're telling a short story.

Suspense
Adding in your senses helps build suspense in your story. So what can you hear, touch, taste, smell, whether it's about you or a character within your story? It helps your audience feel like they're there because they're imagining that they can hear or touch or taste or smell the same things. For example, if you're describing standing outside a room that's full of strangers because you're just about to walk into a network meeting. You could just say you're nervous. Alternatively you could say ' I felt a bead of sweat slowly run down my forehead and along my cheek because I realised the nerves were building. My hands were shaking as I could hear the wall of sound that I was just about to walk into.'

Humour

This is not about becoming a stand-up comic overnight. In fact, if humour is not a strong, part of your personality, doing your best to be funny can fall flat. However, you can be strategic about how you're use as it as it helps to make your story more enjoyable, memorable and definitely relatable. Care has to be taken about timing, tone and target. Because it can backfire on you if you're being inappropriate or excessive. So the guidelines are that humour should relate to the topic you're talking about, definitely be consistent with your personality, and showing respect for your audience. Because remember, you want to make your audience laugh, not cringe.

During the time you were telling your story, make sure to vary your tone, rhythm, and pacing to create dynamic storytelling that holds the audience's attention right from start through to the very end.

Absolutely and wholeheartedly recommend to use anecdotes, anecdotes, and anecdotes to illustrate your key points and add richness and depth to your story.

The most crucial element has to be emotion. The best way to do this is show the emotion, not just talk about it. For example, how does the body or face change when experiencing that particular emotion? So building on what I said about earlier in terms of standing outside a room full of strangers, I could say 'I was very nervous'. But that's talking about the emotion and not showing it. Instead, I might say something like 'my hands started shaking uncontrollably. And then I felt my head start to shake too'.

It's a small difference, but it helps you start to visualize the story. Some starters for ten include

Anxiety - shaking hands, fast breathing, head shaking uncontrollably

Embarrassed - blushing, holding back tears, looking down at the ground

Excited. Breathing more quickly, heart pumping faster, hands thrown up in the air

Hopefully you get the idea.

Just before you go, I want you to talk about how you open up your talk. Those first few moments are really important to engage straight away with your audience.

The core thing to remember is it's about them and not you. Please don't fall into the trap of waxing lyrical about yourself first. I appreciate that you'll want to show that you're credible in front of your audience, but talking about you, your background, and your experience first is not the ideal way to do this. As you will watch your audience switch off one by one.

Another rabbit hole you can fall down is the thank you. Thank you to the person who was introduced you. Lengthy thank you to the person who has invited you to come along. Lengthy thank you to the audience for sitting there and wanting to hear what you're going to say. Just like talking about you, it's likely to send the audience being very interested in scribbling to start scrolling through their phones.

How about instead of focusing on your audience first? Showing them straight out of the gate the reason why they should care about what you're talking about. Because it's all about them.

Showing you get the people in the audience is a great start, especially if you've been in their shoes. But even if you haven't, you can still relate to them by talking about what they care about. For example, what they struggling with or what are their desires or their challenges? Linked with your ability to show them that you've got solutions.

You want your audience to be nodding along. When you see that, you know you've had a great opening. You can actually say things like, ' ah, I can see you nodding along' or 'I'm betting you're nodding yes, in your head'.

Remember, the audience doesn't care about you until they know you care about them. Who you are, where you come from, what you've done, what you've achieved is not important at the beginning. As your audience is much more worried about you wasting their time.

Once you've grabbed their attention and got a positive reaction then you can say who you are. Because at that point they will could be interested to learn more about you and what you do.

Something that can affect your ability to grab attention is whether you have slides or not. I've already talked about not having lots and lots of words on a slide because it becomes a complete distraction. But the same can be true of images. Because you are providing a visual representation that you like instead of letting your audience visualize the picture for themselves.

For example, if I were to talk about my granddad who had a major influence over me growing up, I could show you a photo of him in his three-piece suit and his's pork pie hat so you know exactly who I'm talking about. But that's going to constrain your imagination.

Instead, it is much more powerful for me to describe what my grandad looks like, because you'll start to picture him in your own mind and connect it with images of your granddad, if you were lucky enough to have one, or of older gentleman. So suddenly my story is linked to your imagination, which can be incredibly powerful for you to remember it.

It is your choice whether to use visuals and/or words, just consider whether they will constrain your audience's attention or not.

Finally, the top three questions you can ask to help you select your stories are

1. Knowing what pivotal moments or experiences to share - if you want to tell your origin story as in why you started your business, a great way to start is to bullet point things that have happened since you first made the decision. You can do it chronologically to make things easier, so if you think about different time periods, it might be easier to capture those main points. You can then review each line to think how powerful telling a story around that specific point or a series of points could be

2. How to convey challenges, to be relatable and engaging - linked to the storytelling techniques, think about the emotions you went through when going through that specific challenge. Great way to connect to your audience because they are likely to have gone through those emotions themselves or can relate

3. What aspects of your story will resonate and align with the event theme - where you need a stock of stories to be able to choose from dependent upon the message you want to put across. And going through the 1st question will help you to do this because you will have ended up with a whole list of situations

The Storytelling Sorcerer Guide provided will act as a great foundation on which to select the stories you have in your arsenal to choose from.

Summary

Point A: Telling your story that bores your audience and everyone is checking their phones
Point B: Crafting a compelling story that mesmerises your audience and they are hanging on your every word

Chapter 7: Stage Presence Mastery

How do you feel when you have to talk about yourself and your business to impress a room? I am guessing sweaty palms, hand shaking and possibly finding the floor unusually interesting may be some of the impacts.

Hands up, who loves public speaking? Based on it being the most common fear and ahead of even fear of death, I am guessing you may not be vigorously nodding your head. Especially as most of us would rather jump off a tall building, be surrounded by spiders and even the thought of dying is more acceptable!!

It even has a fancy name, glossophobia, and affects up to 70% who worry about being judged and negatively evaluated by others.

But there's real power to be gained by tapping into the ability to speak, whether in small groups or on a stage, to grow your business. And to grow it at a much faster rate than if you keep hiding.

I get it's scary, trust me, I know. As someone who has introverted qualities, I completely get the fear you experience whilst standing outside a room of strangers, knowing that you're going to be walking in and speak in front of them. Already second guessing yourself and what you're going to say or that just the thought of standing on a stage sends you into a panic.

I remember the first time I had to speak in front of a group. It was only three months into my corporate career. And myself along with the other management graduates were tasked with presenting what we learned in our first three months on the job. Bear in mind this was in front of a board of high-level executives. Where each of us, and there were five of us, were annihilated as we were told how rubbish we had been. Imagine how scarring that was fresh into our careers.

Unfortunately for me speaking has always been a non-optional part of my job. And the more I got promoted, the more I ended up having to speak, often in front of very large audiences, sometimes 500 and more.

Now please don't get me wrong because I was offered a lot of support and training, including professional media training to be able to do all of this. However, the inner shy 6-year-old never disappeared. Every time I had to do it, I could feel the nerves starting as soon as I was told whereas and when I'd be speaking.

I can still remember how much my hands would shake and then my heads would shake and I was convinced the audience would think I was more of a nodding dog than a presenter. But apparently no one ever realised because I had the ability to mask it.

Today is a very different story. Because today, I'm not forced to speak to small groups or on podcasts, or even stand on stages in front of big audiences. It is now a choice and a pleasure because I know it has a positive impact on the audiences I speak to.

124

So please as you going through this chapter be aware you may find it triggers you on your levels of anxiety about speaking, please remember that this is about growing your business in an effective way as well as having that positive impact on your audience. Aand helping make your customers lives better.

You may not realise this, but everybody suffers from anxiety when speaking in public. Even the most professional and best speakers.

One of the most effective ways to help is talking to yourself. I don't mean out loud. I mean I'm in using your inner voice, the voice in your head that's your constant narrative. To remind yourself why you want to do this, why you want to speak in front of others, and as importantly, why you're so passionate about it.

Also, this might sound strange one, but don't run through what you're going to say right before you do it. I don't know about you but it's something I remember doing as a child, before any test. I'd quickly run through my notes beforehand. Just in case I can cram a few last little bits of information in my brain.

But in this circumstance, running through something you're just about to say. What that actually does is sends a message to your brain, that you're not prepared. Now logically you will know that this is the case because you are prepared. The problem is when you keep going over the information, you will build up your anxiety levels. And remember, you will have practiced, practiced, and practiced this so you wouldn't know it by heart. So instead of cramming in the last few minutes, relax, because you've got this.

If it helps and you can do it, visualising what you'll look like on the stage will be a better action. Imagine being in front of those people, engaging with them. They're asking you questions and you know how to answer with absolute confidence because you're so prepared. Then everyone being so entertained, informed and inspired that you get a round of applause at the end.

Doing that is going to be much more powerful than reading over your notes again and again.

The biggest lessons I learned are. The more you present. It's slightly easier it. It gets. Please don't get me wrong, the nerves might still be there. But you can help them by being really prepared and structured in your approach. Which means your confidence will absolutely grow. This is not about winging it. Because if you do that, you won't communicate your message very well and you won't know whether your message is landing and you'll potentially lose your audience. This will create frustration both for you and also the people listening to you. It also won't help with your confidence level and your ability to deliver it and grow your business.

On the subject of being prepared, you can never practice too many times. You might think you could be too

126

prepared, but that's not the case at all. When it comes to speaking in front of other people, the more practiced and prepared you are, the better. Say what you were going to say while you're doing everyday tasks is beneficial. Whether it's washing crockery, ironing, having a bath or sitting on a train, it all helps. Mainly because you're going to sound more natural.

It is not about memorising your talk as this could make you sound artificial. Particularly because the way we speak and the way we write are different. It is the reason I always recommend you read out loud whatever you've just written, to check it sounds like something you would say.

Much better is to remember keywords and phrases that will prompt in your head what the main point is that you want to talk about.

So this chapter is all about Stage Presence Mastery. The ability to be confident in your stage presence, to turn those strangers in your audience into raving fans. Without experiencing paralyzing stage fright.

The three learning outcomes are

1. Overcome stage fright and nervousness and replace them with confidence and charm. So that you can learn the tools that will help you deal with nerves, that may never go away, but will become manageable as you develop more confidence

2. How to establish rapport and build connections that foster trust and engagement. These are crucial elements for you to be successful in generating new customers and sales

3. How to use stagecraft to maintain interest so your audience are willing to walk over hot coals to buy from you

This chapter focuses on how your master the stage, whatever its size. Whether you are looking at small groups or networks for INITIATION, developing your own events MOMENTUM or using other people's stages for MASTERY, the same principles apply. Because whether it is a small audience, your audience or someone else's, the anxiety you go through feels the same.

And remember, this is about growing your confidence, because it's not about whether you are naturally confident or not. because it is something that you can develop over time. The more you do this, the more confident you can become.

Confidence is not about your natural ability to speak in public.

Confidence is not about believing you can succeed at public speaking.

However, the more familiar you become with the process of being able to speak in front of others, you more you get used to it (well that is the idea anyway!).

Think about famous singers who play to huge arenas in front of thousands and thousands of people. Do you really think that they started out with the inherent confidence to be able to stand up in front of all of those people? More likely they started playing small venues and built up their confidence over time. So that as they became more successful, they become more confident in being able to perform in front of huge audiences.

For the purposes of talking to you now, I am suggesting you start off with small groups of like-minded people and your target customer. They are already a friendly audience for you and will be willing you to do well. And once you gain confidence through doing this the opportunities are amazing. Which includes your ability to choose whether you want to speak on big stages or not.

Or even starting out in front of family and friends if that feels more comfortable initially.

OK, let's take a bit of a pause because I appreciate you still may be struggling on getting your head around the ability to do this. These may include

1. Feeling sick with stage fright - your ability to even walk into the room, let alone speak. Coping mechanisms here are to remind yourself of why you're doing this. Why do you want to speak in front of that small group? Why do you want to speak on a podcast to reach a bigger audience? Or why do you want to stand on somebody

else's stage to reach a whole new audience? This is about you growing your business and making a bigger impact

2. Struggling with anxiety to remain focused - the more rehearsed you are, the more likely to be able to cope better. But the time you're doing this you should have been through what you're going to say multiple times. Which enables what you're going to say to flow more effectively and give you confidence. Plus, you can be honest with your audience and they will appreciate your openness. And most people fear public speaking over death!! So most will be sitting there impressed by the fact you're able to speak in front of them

3. Fearing making mistakes in front of an audience - the biggest thing to remember here is your audience have no idea what it is you are going to say. So even if you miss out sections or fluff up sentences or don't quite structure it as you planned, they will never know. And if it helps, use notes. This can be as simple as bullet points on small cards that you can hold. Which you may never even need to refer to, but if it helps with your confidence then do it. Please don't have a script. If you read from the page, it will not come across naturally and you might as well just hand out your notes for everybody to read. Engagement will also be a lot lower than if you're speaking from your heart

As a side note, as I appreciate how much of a barrier this is, one other action you can take is to practice in front of a friendly audience. Asking them for a critique of what worked well and what could be improved, although may

130

feel uncomfortable, is a great way to not only practice but refine what you are going to say.

Think about Olympian champions who practice their skills every single day, with the aim of winning the big event every four years. They do not wait until the last minute to rock up and hope for the best. They put in hundreds and thousands of hours of practice before they even quality for the event.

'Practice makes perfect' but also practice helps to reduce the nerves because you know that you know your stuff so just have to focus on reducing your nerves on the day.

Feeling nervous is a natural emotion and stems from our fight or flight response. We've been hardwired over time to flee from any kind of threat. And standing in front of all of those eyes, no matter how small or big the group is, can trigger your urge to run away.

Even the friendliest of audiences can trigger this response. Think about if you were. If you're on your own and suddenly faced with a lion coming towards you. Straight away your adrenaline kicks in and your heart starts pumping faster. Your body wants to get more oxygen into your blood, into your muscles because you need to be able to either fight the lion (unlikely) or more likely, try to outrun it (which in reality is also unlikely!). So here in that situation it's a great thing to do. However, we get exactly the same response in our body when we speak in public, which is not so great.

The great news is though, that when you know you're fearful of something. You have more of an ability to control it. In this case, whether it's a lion or public speaking. So here are a few ideas for you

Drink water - it may sound simple, but it helps you stop getting a dry mouth. There's nothing worse than going to speak and not being able to get your words out

Move around - it may sound strange, but it's a great way to get rid of any adrenaline that's building up in your system. Given marching up and down on the spot is helpful but ideally to have a bit of a walk around

Power pose - as I will mention again in this chapter, stand like Wonder Woman and drink ining all that superhero energy

Deep breathing - the standard breathing in for four and out for six. But sometimes thinking numbers can make you more anxious, 'how long do I leave between numbers, how fast do I count them, etc. The magic is making the outbreath longer than the in breath.

Interaction - the sooner you get your audience to take action or to speak, the sooner you will start to calm down. This can be in the form of asking questions, getting your audience to stand up and do something or be controversial. All the tactics to instantly engage

Hopefully you're still with me because now I'm going to get into the nitty gritty of how you master that stage presence.

Mastering body language is a great place to start. And this is before you even walk into the room where you do a Power Pose. This always reminds me of Wonder Woman because you stand with feet apart and hands on hips, imagining you are a superhero. Or you can outstretch your hands upwards so you form a V shape. It is great at giving you that millisecond burst of confidence. Because remember, superheroes can take on the world.

Once you're inside the room, it is about maintaining a good posture and standing tall because that conveys confidence and authority. And make sure you're smiling because that shows you are friendly and approachable.

This is effective whether you've just walked into a local network meeting, just about to talk to a small group or indeed go and stand on a stage. It is about giving that air of confidence and approachability.

When you're talking, use gestures purposefully to emphasise the key points and engage with your audience. If, like me, you talk with your hands a lot, then use your hands. Otherwise you'll come across as stilted and you just won't feel like yourself.

Making lots of eye contact with your audience members will help you establish rapport and connection. And remember to keep that smile. Really effective in small

133

groups because everybody will feel engaged. But I appreciate with the bigger audience this is slightly more complex due to the numbers, however, the same principle applies. It is all about your warm and welcoming personality shining through.

If you're standing, remove purposely around the area or stage to maintain energy and keep the audience's attention. And whether you're sitting or standing, think about the visual aids that you're using. For example, in a small group, I print onto cards any key visuals that I want to use to emphasize the points I'm making. And on a formal stage consider whether it's just you speaking to the audience or whether you want to use the screen to show visuals. If yes, please don't overload with words and my recommendation is to purely use images (especially as we are much more likely to remember images than any words).

Having space on a stage means you can transition between different areas. Your ability to walk from the left hand into the middle to then the right hand of the stage means that more of the audience will be able to see you.

The next element is your ability to develop an emotional connection with the audience. This is the game changer. Where you have the ability to use your voice to secure new customers and sales.

Linking back to Storytelling Sorcerer, your ability to share personal anecdotes, stories or examples will help you create that all important emotional connection. And I know it's a cliché and we do love them in marketing, 'know, like, trust' is possible to achieve through speaking in a group. That emotional connection will help your audience to get to know you by the by the stories you share. And your ability to be entertaining, engaging and informative will help them like you. Which then leads to the all-important trust factor.

That emotional connection gives you a great platform for you to promote your offer. Well, if you've done a great job in the room by showing who you are, what you do, and for who, you have the ability to sell in the room as well.

This is all underpinned by you showing genuine enthusiasm, passion and empathy for your topic to inspire and engage your audience. Strength of your personality is what will shine through and connect in a deep way.

The third and final element is how effectively you engage with your audience. Most people will start with saying who they are, what they do, and why they're here. How refreshing instead, to ask your audience questions. Engaged from the beginning. Because they won't care who you are, what you do, and why you're there until they're engaged and care.

It is time well spent to consider what the key struggles or desires of your audience are. And then use those to ask questions. For example, if I'm in front of a group of female business owners, I can pose 3 questions and ask for raised hands to show response

1. Who is passionate about what they do?

2. Who would like a few more customers and sales?

3. Who feels like a best kept secret?

I thank them for their response, where most of the audience have put their hands up, and explain I wanted to check to make sure I was in the right place which normally results in laughter. At that point, I can explain who I am, what I do, and why I'm there.

A simple change to the traditional format, but with the ability to make an impact from the beginning.

Because encouraging audience interaction will result in higher engagement. There's nothing worse than having to sit there and listen to somebody talk, where you are expected just to sit there and listen. How many times have you found yourself in that situation? And how much of what that person said can you remember?

There is real power in encouraging audience interaction through questions, polls or activities to keep them actively involved.

And using humorous anecdotes or rhetorical questions will capture more attention and stimulate interest.

136

This may be the hardest step to overcome. And I so appreciate how difficult it is to speak in front of a group, no matter how small. I have been through it and still go through the nerves even today.

But the difference is I now choose to speak in groups and in front of big audiences. Because I know how powerful it is for my business to speak to my target customer, in a way that they can get to know me and the genuine reasons behind why I do what I do.

And part of being prepared is understanding that things could go wrong, and it's how you deal with those situations. Sometimes your mind might go blank right before you're about to speak, or even in the middle of it. This is a natural situation because our bodies are in state of stress which triggers our fight or flight response.

It might help to remember when this happens that it's because back in the day when we were Cavemen hunting, we'd have this response to get away from Saber-tooth tigers. Funnily enough, today, we don't have to worry about that and reminding ourselves of that fact will, one, make you smile, and two, hopefully help you calm down.

Because our bodies are designed to survive. And when we go into this mode, everything in our body is focused on getting the energy to be able to run. The last thing your body is going to be worried about is your short-term memory. One of the reasons why people sometimes can't remember a traumatic incident.

The same can happen just before you're about to speak. So as well as reminding yourself there are no tigers inside, do your power poses and breathe deeply.

How you present yourself when both sitting and standing is an important reflection of your confidence.

Posture - important as it projects a positive image to your audience. When standing, make sure your feet are hip distance apart as this is a really solid position. And gives you a solid base from which to walk around from and she should be able to move naturally from one spot to another

Breath - being able to take a calm and deep breath will give you energy in your voice. Will also help you deal with nerves before entering the room or the stage

Voice - it might seem a little strange, but you have two different voices, the one you project from your chest and the one you project from your head. The chest is deeper but harder to project, making the one from the head easier to amplify. How can you tell the difference? Put one hand on your chest and the other one on the top of your head. Now say the word 'oooh' and feel the vibration in your chest. If you do the same thing but using a higher pitch sound you'll feel it in your head. It is an exercise that singers use and can work as well for when you're speaking as it helps you with projecting your voice and finding your natural pitch

Something to bear in mind is the natural level of your voice. For example, if you're softly spoken, it may be difficult for some people to hear you even in a small room. This is where vocal aids such as microphone may be useful

Eye contact - your audience will want you to look at them. It also helps with your energy levels as you feel the reactions and engagement of your audience. I'm not talking about looking straight into people's eyes, you can look just over their heads if you were at all nervous. And please don't be affected by people's reactions, for example, if someone who looks bored or tired, because you have no idea what's going on in their lives. Their reaction may have nothing to do with you whatsoever.

A general rule is to be able to look in all directions. Starting from left through to middle through to right. So you're scanning the whole room. In contrast, it just to picking a point and just staring at that which will be really off putting for anybody in the audience.

In a small room, you have the ability to make eye contact with every other person in the room, change your focus from one to another. But obviously in a bigger room is a little bit more challenging so the objective is to make eye contact with as many as you can

Body language - if you naturally speak with your hands, then please continue to speak with your hands. There's nothing worse than somebody trying to keep their arms down by their sides when that isn't their natural way of body language. Being open armed is a positive approach. In essence, this is about you behaving naturally and not using artificial language because you want to come across as more energetic or extrovert. And it goes without saying, things like putting your hands in pockets or folding your arms is not a great way to engage with your audience

My final thought relates to the things that make you, you. Including the way you speak and the accent that you have. I can say this because I have a West Midlands accent. And I remember very clearly moving down to London after graduation and being faced with people he thought I spoke in a funny way. The most memorable was the way that I pronounce 'bus' which sounds a bit like 'buzz'. What I would often hear the phrase, ' sorry, what is a buzz, ah, you mean a bus'.

As you can imagine, that was the tip of the iceberg.

When I speak, I could worry about how other people judge me for the way that I speak. But truth bomb time. And don't care about the way you speak. It's about the content that you're giving them that they're interested in. They want to know what you've got to say and the value you're going to provide to them. No matter what your accent is.

Even if you are self-conscious, they won't be!

140

Whatever size stage you're thinking about, whether it's a small network group, putting on your own event or speaking of somebody else's stage, please consider this...

Imagine taking onto that stage fully confident you can own that space. Where you are seen as an expert in what you do. And customers flock to buy from you.

How great would that feel?

Now you can use the Stage Presence Mastery Checklist to identify what you need to do to grow in confidence.

In summary
Point A: suffering with off the chart anxiety and stage fright, just at the thought of speaking
Point B: Being confident and gloriously visible on every stage to increase your credibility without a flicker of fear

Chapter 8: Connection Queen

It never ceases to fascinate me when I have conversations with female business owners about how they leverage either attempting or speaking to groups, whether they're small or large. Because the number of times when I ask how many inquiries or how much business do you generate from spending your time with those groups, the answer is often 'minimal'. But when I asked them why do they keep doing it, responses 'I know that networking is good for my business' or 'because speaking to groups is something that I need to do to get my business in front of more people.'

Yet, if the results are so low, is this really the best use of your time? My answer would be yes if you leverage each of the opportunities. My answer would be yes if you have a purpose behind every time you step into the room. My answer would be yes if you track the impact of each opportunity.

Please don't get me wrong, I fully realise that spending time with like-minded women is an absolute bonus. Also a great way to get away from the isolation that can be a result of working on your own. So from a mental health perspective, it is exceptionally positive. And I fully appreciate that this is a purpose in itself which I would never underestimate.

For the purposes of this chapter, I am talking about the objective of growing your business utilising these opportunities, which results in a variety of outcomes.

1. Generating new connections - the ability to add to your audience and, to have nurturing those relationships.

2. Generating income - a powerful message shared in the room can not only generate a new lead, but result in sales

3. Identifying new collaborations - a great platform to meet like-minded individuals who share your beliefs and values, who could be great partners in new business opportunities

It is why this section is all about how to leverage connections, conversation and chemistry to turn leads into paying prospects without manipulating or pressuring them.

The 3 learning outcomes are

1. How to influence decision making and buying behaviour to gain trust. This is a fundamental marketing activity, whatever action you're taking, in this case, leveraging your voice but also as important across the marketing channels you choose to leverage

2. How to build genuine connections to lay the foundation for successful conversion. Genuine is crucial here. It is not about using people because you think they might come in use further down the line. This is about being who you are and showing that you value the relationship

146

3. How to master persuasive communication techniques to enable leads and successfully position solutions. This extends across everything that you say in person, but also in writing or video. Especially in this case because this methodology includes securing opportunities to speak as well as being front of those groups whether small or large. Your ability to deeply connect through a pitch document to secure an opportunity is the start point here

Building, growing and leveraging connections may seem daunting, but fundamentally it's about building friendships. If you view it in this way, it should make it slightly less daunting. Especially if you think about one of the analogies that I often use about coffee shop to illustrate making a connection.

Imagine walking into a very busy coffee shop, you look around and there's only one empty chair left, that is on the table for two where one person is already sitting there. So you collect your beverage of choice and walk over, to tentatively ask ' if this seat is free, do you mind if I take it?'. With the hopeful reply of ' yes, please do', when you smile, sit down and introduce yourself and ask what their name is.

You notice the person has a laptop so you might ask if they're there to work. They explain yes, because they're fed up with working from home, especially because it's only them. As it turns out, they're a business owner like you. So that starts a whole conversation about working from home and the pros and cons. By the end, he arranged to meet the same time next week. When you bring your laptop and you become business buddies.

Now, using the same scenario, what do you think would have happened if you sat down and said ' buy my stuff', 'buy my stuff, no, really, buy my stuff' or in this situation if the connection iss so you can develop speaking opportunities, you might say, 'I want to speak at your event'!

The former is more likely to secure your connection, then turning to an opportunity. Whereas the second scenario you are just likely to put that person off.

How about deploying this approach to making connections, where you are able to leverage conversations and chemistry, develop opportunities that are beneficial for both of you. Without manipulation or pressure.

Because this is about building genuine connections to lay the foundation for successful conversion of opportunities. And all without feeling spammy.

But you may be thinking at this point, 'that all sounds great, but how am I going to do it?'. Well, first thing to realize is what might hold you back

1. Overcoming the fear of rejection and awkward interactions. It is easy to go down this rabbit hole and fill yourself with self-doubt. Where you ask yourself questions like 'why would they be interested?', 'what would make

148

them want to learn more about me?' or 'am I good enough?'. I'm guessing these are familiar sentences which you ask yourself in lots of different situations. For the purposes of these connections, how about focusing on your opportunity to make a bigger impact, to help more people through what you do. Certainly, it's no longer about you and you know you can talk passionately about the customers that you help

2. Sustaining meaningful conversations to keep them flowing. Ah, that sounds a bit fancy, doesn't it? What I mean is engaging for the long term. Don't treat every new connection as an immediate opportunity. Instead, value it as a new relationship which is balanced for both of you. So you can genuinely be yourself because you connect through values and beliefs

3. Feeling huge discomfort in having to self-promote yourself. Linked to This is not about you in isolation, growing your business so you can help even more and have a ripple effect on even more people than that. And fundamentally, if you don't toot your own horn, who is going to? You are passionate about what you do and provide a product or service that your customers benefit from. But if no one knows about you, you won't be able to have the impact that you desire

Building quality connections is so much more fulfilling than quantity, especially when you are not the loudest in the room. Your preference, if it's anything like mine, is small group settings. Initially, you might be better off rather than

149

attending large networking events, to grow deep relationships through groups and networks. The result being to create a supportive network of individuals who value you.

Leveraging your natural ability to listen, empathise and build deep connections means you can build confidence by thinking ahead, practicing your pitch, and focusing on what value you can provide in the group.

And those active listening skills are paramount because it gives you the ability to summarise what the other person has shared with you, showing you've taken the time to understand and hear them. Alongside asking relevant questions to gain more insight, enabling you to build rapport.

Empathy is also great to build trust as you connect much more on a deeper emotional level.

You have a fantastic opportunity to cultivate a very close network of really genuine connections, investing time in nurturing those relationships, just like you should be doing with your existing audience.

Including reaching out to offer support and showing genuine interest in them, not just their businesses, but what's happening in their personal lives.

In essence, being who you are. With the opportunity here of building a really strong support group and who knows what can happen in terms of opportunities?

The first step is how you can genuinely engage to go beyond surface level.

INITIATION

Three phases are detailed here but this is not an exhaustive list, instead it's meant as a starter, to help you leverage group opportunities and to develop the opportunity to speak in front of them on a topic that will not only engage them but also encourage them to buy from you.

There is an optional phase before the meeting, where you have the opportunity to interact with both the organiser and the other attendees. This is often via an online group linked to the meeting. I am not intending to cover here as there is lots of advice how to interact in online groups, eg share value, respond to comments, ask questions etc. And if there is an opportunity to post in the group, make sure your focus is on your target customer in any content, to engage, add value etc.

The first formal phase is your introduction message. Being in small groups or network events normally provides an opportunity to introduce yourself and your business, often referred to as the 60 second pitch. The standard format is I help X to do Y to achieve Z and there's nothing wrong with that formula at all. But if you want to create an emotional connection straight away it's unlikely to do that.

Instead, there's a very simple three-step formula I've developed as part of the Being Demand methodology

1. Use a question based on the situation that your target customer will recognise. This can be based on a struggle or a desire (I appreciate that most tell you to only focus on struggles but adding in a desire increases the emotional connection)

2. Short sentence to explain who you are and what you do but using very easy to understand language. So your target customer instantly knows what you offer them

3. Example of someone who has benefited from what you offer, providing proof of the positive impact you make

For example, a brand photographer could say

You know how women get photos taken and not use them AT ALL to promote their business because they don't like how they look in them, even thought they are great images.
My name is Rose and I show you how to be relaxed so your images are natural and you cannot wait to share them.
Just like Amy did and got 5 new enquires just because she showed her face.

And then the all-important call to action. What is it you want people to do next.

The best advice I can give here is to practice your message over and over again, when you're in the shower, driving in the car or find yourself on your own for a minute. Because the more you say it, the more you'll refine it and use words that sound natural for you. Which means when you're doing your introduction in a group, you sound natural and therefore genuine.

Now that is normally at the beginning of the session, so the second phase is about interaction and how you eight act in the group. The key here is to ask lots of questions and show how interested you are with the other people in the group, not in an artificial way, just that you genuinely want to know more about them. And in wider group discussions to participate and give your opinions.

I appreciate how challenging this can be. As it can feel daunting even in a small group to speak.

The framework I share with my clients is based on 5 steps but the one I have shared here is effective in getting attention.

Hopefully this will help you because I know how scary it is to open your mouth for the first time. I do my best to be in the room early which means that I can smile and say hello as other women enter the room. It also means I am not walking into room of strangers because I'm already there.

153

And means it is less scary to chat when there are only a couple of women initially before everyone else arrives.

Once it starts, I will remain quiet for a few minutes, allowing my nerves to hopefully subside, and gives me a chance to learn a little bit about the other women in the room. Then when the opportunity arises, I will engage with the conversation. So even if there are lots of loud women in the room, I still have the opportunity to get noticed.

The third phase, which is where a lot of the magic happens is after the meeting. And splits into two areas

1. Follow up with the organiser - a thank you is always welcomed and what you enjoyed about the session. As well as an opportunity to offer to speak at a future event and what you would love to speak on to add value to their group

2. Follow up with attendees - by spending time with the group, you will have identified who are potential new connections for you, with any friendships, potential collaborations or potential customers

As with the coffee shop analogy, these shouldn't be forced. It's about making genuine connections where you can both benefit.

It really is all in the follow up. Making new connections is fantastic but it's then what you do to deepen that connection that will really make a difference.

1. Timing - the quicker you follow up the better. Because this shows the level of respect you have and also your enthusiasm to get to know them more

2. Value - what information could you provide to them that would be really useful. Maybe you did document or a video that you think will be helpful for that person. Or there's someone you would like to connect them to because you think would be a good collaboration for them

3. Intention - share the reason why you would like to get to know them better. Is it because what you do is complementary? Or you think you can be a great support to each other? Or if you think you can help them

And because it really is all about the follow up, tracking what you're doing is really useful. Especially to make sure that you're not hounding the person but are contacting them enough, that in case they're busy, to keep you on their radar.

MOMENTUM

Creating connections for your own events is linked to the above as well as connections you're making through other marketing channels. I'm not going to labour the point here because this is part of your wider strategy to nurture your audience.

The crucial part is utilising your target list to ensure you actively engage and deepen connections with your most

155

potential customers. As this will be the list that you will target in the 'Sold Out Success System' for your own event in the next chapter.

MASTERY

Being a Connection Queen for speaking on other people's stages is super important.

Research is the first step here to identify conferences, events, and organisation that fit with your values. This is about identifying the stages that you want to speak on that are available to speak on that you're interested in. Because you resonate with the people organising. You've already created a powerful speaker profile in 'Profile Architect' that differentiates you from your competition and establishes you as the either go to expert.

In this chapter, it's about identifying who you want to connect with to be able to use that speaker profile.

The number of ways you can make this happen are below to give you options to choose which you feel most comfortable with.

1. Stages you want to speak on - develop your ideal target list and the reasons why you want the opportunity to speak. Initially, reach out to connect with the individual responsible, through their social media profile, if possible, to make a low-pressure connection and start to interact.

This gives you a foundation on which to formally reach out on but consider non-traditional ways to do this.

For example, rather than sending a direct message or e-mail, could you use a different personalised mechanic? For example, a personalised video to explain why you want to contact them, using information about events that they've already run, to establish a start point.

You can then follow up in a non-sleazy way because you don't want them to be on the receiving end of 'did you get my message?' Instead, consider how you can follow up in a non-stalker kind of way. If you get no response, think about focusing on the other targets on your list.

If you get a response, this is where you can use your speaker profile, including the key topics that you think would be relevant to speak on for their audience. Once you get a level of interest you can work out the details of when and how

2. Stages open to pitch - there are a number of organisers who will do a call out for speakers. The easiest way is to do an online search of 'call for speakers', where you will come across opportunities to Eventbrite, local event calendars Ted X, Meet Up etc.

Don't just be constrained by the subject focus of the conference. For example, if you are a finance person, don't just look for finance events and conferences. Because your presence will be welcomed at many different industry conferences and events etc.

Use hashtags to identify your prospect list, for example, #event, #onference, #conference speaker, #xindustryspeaker and if you are looking for local connections #eventlocalarea etc.

The added benefit of using hashtags research means you will automatically be shown opportunities in your feed every day. So it is an easy way to build a system of constantly identifying local event and conference organisers that you want to connect with and build a relationship with.

There are many opportunities at a small local and community level to start off with. It is great practice to move from smaller stages through to being part of panels, to group talks and then to be featured as a speaker.

The key is cultivating relationships with the event organisers and conference directors. Get to know them so you can ask questions about what they look for in a speaker. And what kinds of presentations that their audiences might be interested in?

All this information enables you to get background information which you can then use when you want to formally pitch. And also being on the radar of the event organisers means that they have you on file so that gives you an opportunity for any last minute requirements or substitutions.

To helping you search for stages, develop a calendar of events. These are especially important because some organisers will book speakers many months in advance. So these early actions you can take to build connections and deep relationships, will pay dividends for this. So how about starting your online search now of 'call for speakers' and link it with keywords from your marketplace. Then start reaching out.

Provide information on who you are, what you speak about and how it can help, support and add value to their audience. Then follow up after a few days. And if no reply, wait another week to follow up again. But do not hound them. And if you get no response, wait until the event is a bit closer and try again.

And remember to reach out in advance, maybe 3-6 months before. This is why it is so important to build up your connection and deepen the relationship over time.

But remember, be specific about the audience you want to get in front of so you focus your energy making connections and building relationships with the people that are most relevant for you to achieve your goals.

Be specific on the type of speaking opportunities you're after
1. Small venue and highly engaged people

159

2. Conference venue with a large audience

3. Industry professionals or organisations such as colleges etc

This will help you narrow down your focus. For example, there are very different connections if you want to speak in a local event group of say 30 to wanting to speak at a TEDx conference.

When you are reaching out to make connections, think about if you know anybody that works for the organisation behind the event or if you've attended their event in the in the past. In which case you could explain how their initial eventual conference impacted you and how it made a difference. And when doing this, be specific and personalise the information that you sending directly to that person.

There's no use in using a generic template to send out to make that initial connection. Because that's the fastest way to end up in the bin.

And when you do inquire about the event, but keep it short and ask specific questions that can be answered quickly by them so to not take up a lot of their time. For example, when will you be taking speaker applications for X event? Because it's about being respectful of their time. Rather than getting into story and why they should choose you before you have those initial details.

So it's about who you are, what you speak about, and how you can help their audience and add value.

3. Physically attending conferences and events that you want to speak at -– this is a fantastic way to get to know the organisers, the audience and the person responsible for booking speakers. So it's a great way to make an initial connection. You can follow up with after the event and reach out via social media. Or using direct details if they gave you a business card.

My top tip if you're attending the event is take lots of photographs of you at the event and the event itself and use their hashtag. Because once the event is over, the organisers will search the hashtag they gave out on the day and obviously see that your event, you were at the event and are saying complimentary things about them. Which gives you a great opportunity to reach out to them and say would they like to use your photos that you took on the day.

Imagine how fantastic that is for the person that organised the event or the conference, particularly if it was small and they didn't use professional photographers. So you're giving them real value and they will remember you.

It also gives you an easy way to follow up after the event. Where you can send them a message or an e-mail about your experience, but keep it short. The impact should be a positive one and it's keeping you fresh in that person's mind.

You can also provide a testimonial to them and you say you're more than happy for them to use it across all of their marketing.

4. Join the Speakers Association - probably one of the easiest ways to make and build connections because your part of a like-minded community. An online search will identify both national and also local associations. It has the added benefit of connecting and building deep relationships with people that are more experienced than you are and can help you find even more public speaking opportunities and connections.

Of course, please don't underestimate the power of asking for referrals. For example, going live or speaking in front of your own audience. And then asking for opportunities to connect with event organisers, can pay dividends.

In essence, speaking is a relationship business. The deeper connections that you can nurture, the more successful that you're going to be. Where you get known by the key decision makers and also influencers. For asking you to speak at events, conferences, etc.

5. Venue Managers - one other idea on building deep connections which you may not have considered is local hotels. Getting to know the event manager within the hotel can be a fantastic connection for you. Especially if

they get to know you as a person and what is it you want to achieve so that they can recommend you to organisations that book their venue for any events and conferences.

Ultimately, it is up to you to identify the connections you most want to put energy and focus into.

Because if you are serious about standing on other people's stages, it requires action. And ongoing action. Just making a list will not get you results.

This is about doing the search, making the list and reaching out to build deep relationships. So there is a time commitment, but the dividends it can pay are huge.

Please use the Connection Queen Checklist to identify the actions you need to build your list of potential speaking opportunities.

In summary
Point A: No real connections or booked calls and being too scared to reach out
Point B: Being a connection queen and filling your calendar with ease of speaking opportunities

Chapter 9: Sold Out Success System

Imagine the power of your ability to build your own stage to deliver income and impact success without being a sleazy seller. Where you sell out your own stages. And be seen as the go- to expert enabling you to grow sustainably.

But be aware that there's a lot involved in putting on your own event. As there are a lot of things to think about, whether it's a large venue or a smaller room. The key to everything is planning. And as importantly, planning for any potential surprises.

And this means before you've even decided on a date, booking a venue, sorting out whether you're going to have other speakers and other aspects things like food.

Planning is the key that unlocks the door to your event being sold out, having a room full of very happy attendees. And your ability to sell from that stage.

With the very first step is of being clear in your goals and objectives. As this will help you to stay on track. Remember the purpose of the event and what the expected outcome is for you. Because you want to create an event that's both exciting for the attendees but also income generating for you.

Also, work out whether you are looking to generate income from sale of tickets to the event or to break even. The reason for this is you are unlikely to make high profits from sales of the tickets. So having your focus on the income you can generate on the back of the event will help you shape the event itself.

This is not a vanity project. This is using a marketing tactic to generate income for your business.

The 3 learning outcomes are

1. How to take actions before the event to ensure that you sell out the spaces with your target customer. This is an important point because there's a difference between filling an event with people and filling an event with your target customer base

2. How to leverage the event to sell from the stage. Initially, this links back to being a Storytelling Sorcerer and developing Stage Presence Mastery. However, a core component of that leverage is having an offer that your audience in the room already want. Without that, you won't make sales on the day

3. To follow up with your target audience after the event. For those that don't buy on the day, there is still an opportunity to promote the core offer. But also as importantly, to have a down sell option for them if the core offer is not right for them today

If you want to sell out an event, focus on income is a secondary. The initial focus has to be all about the people. Be focused more on what the outcome is for the people attending. You are much more likely to sell the event out, no matter what the particular price.

Think about all those huge arenas that hold thousands and thousands of people who were all there to see their favourite band. And even those that are right at the back so all they can see is tiny spots on the stage, will crawl over hot coals to be there just to experience the event.

Imagine your ability to do the same thing for your audience, making your event so desirable, they'd trek through jungles to get to it!!

Hang on for a minute. Could it be that you might hold yourself back from doing this? So you may well recognize some of these struggles.

1. Fearing the ability to reach a wider audience - first, you don't need a huge audience. It is much more about their level of engagement and much more likely to be successful if you nurture the audience you have. Secondly, making the event irresistible will automatically get you out to a wider audience. Because not only will your existing audience know about it, but they will tell others. There are tactics you can deploy to gain the interest of brand-new people, for example, a simple one is when anyone books to offer them a reduced price for any friends who buy a second ticket

2. Being worried about selling out the event - your ability to reach a wider audience should reduce the fear on this

one. And fundamentally, it's about having a plan of action as to how you sell the tickets, from having an event that will naturally entice people through to tactics such as using early bird promotion. As you read on, there are a number of tactics that you can deploy, depending upon what you feel comfortable with.

3. Feeling anxious about whether your audiences' expectations will be met - by understanding what it is your audience want through research, you can mitigate this impact. Also planning a fantastic programme for the event based on consistent engagement, means your audience are more likely to be happy

Now, I appreciate that most people don't like selling as it can feel cheesy, even if it's for your own event that you know will be brilliant. But you need to sell in order to sell out your event. But if you start from the point that you truly believe in the event that you are developing and that it will have a positive impact to those coming along, it is a different mindset.

It becomes more about finding people who you want to have this experience. Choosing who you want in the room. And not just hoping anybody buys a ticket. If you're more purposeful in this way, you are much more likely to fill your room with the people that you want there. Those that are likely to want to buy the offer you are going to present to them on the day.

How great would it be for you to be able to sell out every speaking event you develop without feeling sleazy, cheesy or salesy. Knowing you can crush your revenue goals.

So your starting point has to be asking yourself the question of what success looks like. And have you done similar events to this in the past which you can learn from? Tangible goals will include ticket sales, revenue, number of people at the event through to the kind of contact information that you want to capture. Intangibles are more like developing an unforgettable atmosphere, a memorable experience and high event attendees' level of satisfaction.

Next deciding on the killer title for your event so it is an easy decision to buy a ticket.

Because by creating Aa great event title. That alone can draw in event seekers wherever you shout about the event. Remember you are looking to attract your target audience. In contrast too, if your event title is not very exciting, it's not going to grab their attention.

A killer title can help your target customer understand the purpose of your event. And that it's intended for them and what they'll get from joining it. First up, who's your target audience? So who are you trying to target? Why should they attend? And how can you make the event memorable for them?

And the best way to do this is to make the title short and easy to remember. It needs enough details to capture their attention, but in a very specific and succinct way. So that your event title stands out.

If you want to start point, look at other event titles of people from within your marketplace. But also look at other industries as you might find more inspiration there with regard to how they've structured the title or their use of words.

How about drafting your title and sending out to some previous attendees or your target customer within your audience to see what they think the events about? And you're doing it without providing any context other than the event title. And consider original words to use rather than a traditional or generic ones that other people within your marketplace use.

You can also do an online search for 'free event generator title' if you are lacking inspiration. But bear in mind, just like any other free generators, it is only as good as the instructions that you feed it.

Bear in mind that there are lots of different ways to make your event title more interesting and appealing. But this doesn't mean using jargon or buzzwords. And you can use free tools like the Hemingway app online which will tell you what the reading level of your event title is. Because Marketing 101 will tell you to aim your content at an 11-year-old.

The guidelines I would give you is to make sure that within your event title you focusing on the outcome for the attendees. How will they benefit from joining your event? Because this is about selling the experience and the outcome, not just the event itself.

And a great way to make sure your event title is clear and also concise is to read it out loud. Is it easy to read? Do you instantly understand it? Does it make you feel excited and want to attend the event?

Because what you want is to create a feeling of excitement. What is it your target customer wants to hear? Put yourself in their shoes and think about how they would describe your event if somebody asked them to explain what it was in one sentence.

For example, for a marketing workshop
Option 1: Learn the marketing tips to help you grow your business

Option 2: Learn how to create demand for what you do so you sell out again and again

Option 2 is focused on what the outcome is for the attendee and will appeal to my target customer as I know they want to sell out.

After deciding on a killer title for your event, next up, although you might feel a bit uncomfortable, is getting loud.

173

Shout about what you're going to cover, what you're going to speak about, about the sessions you're going to have in the event and shout about the amazing takeaways your attendees will walk away with.

Show them what return on investment they're going to get.

So back to not feeling comfortable. When I talk about getting loud, I'm not talking about shouting or being the largest in the room, because, I don't know about you, but for me that would be really uncomfortable, I don't know about you. Instead, it is about deploying multiple communication tools through multiple marketing channels. But only using marketing channels you are comfortable with. So for example, if doing lives (as in live videos) is not your comfort zone, then it shouldn't go on the list. Because you would come across as uncomfortable and not be able to convert people effectively.

For the purpose of your own events, I'm going to cover Initiation and Momentum (Mastery is about other people's stages so not as relevant here.

INITIATION

This covers smaller, more intimate events. For example, in 2022 I set up my own network community, where each month I put on a mini event that I spoke at. This was an Opportunity to showcase other women in the room as well as promote myself and my business.

The outcome was that it helped the growth of my business, but it also helped the growth of those women who attend. Simply because you have the know, like and trust factor in the room.

If you decide to set up a network, it has to be something that you commit both time and effort to. Just expecting to build a group and that they will all come would be naive. It takes a similar process to filling a larger event, to make a smaller event effective. So you constantly have to promote filling your network event every single month. It is not a decision to be taken lightly and has asked to form part of the core of your marketing strategy.

Here are a few things to consider when setting up and running your own network group to create leads and sales

1. Clearly define goals. For example, to bring like-minded people together who share similar values goals

2. Define who you want there and the size of the network events. You want a mix of returning women, but also the ability to attract new faces as well so you are constantly refreshing the group

3. Structure. Is it formal or casual? How will you lead the meetings? How frequently will they take place? What outcomes are you going to provide for the group?

4. Frequency. Define how often the group meets and make sure it's consistent

5. Communication. The ability to contact individuals outside of the network event

And remember, successful networks are as much about listening and research as doing. To provide a regular event that constantly sells out there, has to be a reason for those people to want to be in the room. And are all covered under Momentum so you can use the same principles for your own network event.

Constantly focus on what success looks like for you. Because the effort and energy to sell out your small event each month has to correlate the return on investment for you.

MOMENTUM

First step before you do anything is coming up with the theme or message of your event

How do you want to attract attendees in the first place?

What do you want them to do in the event?

What do you want them to do after leaving the event?

Also what kind of event do you want to develop? Is it an educational one? Is it an inspirational one?

176

And are you going to promote your offer throughout event or do you want to be more subtle and focus the event on gathering leads that you can sell something to attendees after the event.

Next is who's the event for?

Being clear on your target customer will help you plan to sell out the event for that specific audience. Then you can think about things like venue and dates.

When you're developing your own events, you have a choice to make, for you to be the solo speaker or for you to bring in other speakers. In the case where there are speakers, your decision is do you pay or not pay for their time? Well known speakers who will help you attract people to the event will have to be paid. Which includes paying for them to be there, but also potentially their travel and accommodation.

Where you are not paying fees, there is still a huge benefit to that other person as they're getting exposure to your audience. When you're selecting speakers and/or all facilitators, think about their level of influence and knowledge. Be supercritical about how they're going to align with you and your audience.

What about interactive elements and breaks? If you have more than you speaking, for example, multiple speakers, how about Q&A sessions or panel discussions? And putting in sufficient breaks in order to foster interaction and prevent fatigue during the day. Because you want to keep the energy levels as high as you can.

In this case, though, there are a few things to consider
1. Size of their audience - do they have a reasonably sized and an engaged audience? But even more importantly, are they your target customer?

2. Values - do they share your values and beliefs? This is a really important one, as you need to be able to work with this person, and for them to understand what it is you are looking to achieve

3. Commitment - are they willing to promote your event to their audience? You need to gain their commitment to get loud about your event. You can help them do this by providing marketing collateral material that they can use

There are logistics to consider as well. For example, whether you provide food or not. If it's a day event, you want everybody to stay for lunch because you want them to be able to connect network but also for you to be able to promote your offer.

You will cover this as part of the venue conversation. What's included and what's not? For example, as well as food and refreshments. How about tech? Is that covered? And I definitely suggest visiting the venue more than once, first time to check it out and negotiate. But then to go back and work out the logistics of the room, not just table setup, but actually how do you want to dress the room for impact?

And not to underestimate the help that you might need. Do you need help beforehand? Does anybody else need to be there on the day to help you? And if yes, do you want them to wear branded T-shirts?

If you do want volunteers, how about making it a little more exciting and create an application for them to fill out? As it means you can ask people from within your audience to do it. Here it is great to consider the kind of benefits you can give them. For example, some will volunteer to get free ticket, some just want to support you, some will just want to be helpful.

And how about treating it like a marketing activity. So initially reach out to people you think will be interested. And from a timing perspective, the sooner you get the communication out there, the better as they'll help you promote the event and it gives you time to get to know them and their skill sets.

Only from a logistics perspective, what kind of marketing collateral do you need? From a standard item such as brochures, leaflets, exhibition stand. Through to how are you going to market the room itself? For example, do you want branded marketing displays.

How about logistics on the day? These might seem minor actions in the grand scheme, but in order for you to be successful at selling from the stage, you need to make sure it's the best experience possible for your audience.

Including who's going to be what on the day. For example, registration as to who will tick everybody off the list, especially as that's the first point of contact for many people. For tech who's making sure that everything runs smoothly? Who will make sure that everything runs to plan on the day? Through to things like making sure the goodie bags are there.

And just picking up on plans for the day, what do you want your event to look like? Think about events that you've been to and what made them special. Why do people keep going back there? For example, it's an opportunity to put names in a hat where the winners get 3 minutes on the stage and maybe there are three spots in the morning, three in the afternoon.

How are you going to balance educational and networking components? For example, having combination of speaking, splitting into smaller groups, networking breaks.

Also super important to consider people's sensory needs. For example, having quiet areas allowing people get away from the main group if they want to.

Each element forms part of the overall experience.

Once you have decided on those and what your overall theme for the event is you will then be in a position to action the next part, how to sell tickets?

When selling tickets think about timing. Not just in your diary, but also in the diary of the people you're going to target to join you. Because they need to block it out in their diary, so make sure you're giving them enough notice. Also to give them time to plan things like booking travel, possibly accommodation.

You have already defined what your goal is, as in how many people you want there, what the purpose of it is. So now you can map it out just like any other marketing activity. I recommend you treat it like you would the launch of any new offer. You need activity to get enough eyes on you so that you sell the number of tickets you want to? Please don't underestimate the amount of energy and time needed, because you have to heavily promote the event, to cut through all the noise.

For example, if your event is a month away, have activity planned for every week. Each week and deploy a ed different activity to incentivize people to sign up for your event. And remember the quicker you people to sign up, that more people there are to promote you.

The ways to help you sell out your event are

Previous event attendees - go back out to the attendees. These are likely to be your biggest supporters and are more likely to immediately purchase the event tickets. And you're showing them that you appreciate them by offering them a special price for signing up early and quickly

Target list – think about who you want to join you. Reach out to people on your target list. It can be amazing the response you get through a personalised invitation. Especially if you link it with, 'you are the first to know'

Hot targets – previous customers, existing customers, network, engage in content, free event attendees and ambassadors

Warm targets – email list, social media followers, event no shows, collaborators

Cold targets – other people's audiences, new followers, people you have identified to want to buy from you

Early bird pricing. It is standard tactic to have two prices, early bird and then ongoing. You can also have different types of early bird, pre-early bird and early bird to encourage people to buy tickets for the event before the price increases again. It gives you a sense of urgency that encourages people to buy sooner

Ask early ticket buyers to promote the event - they are likely to be your best supporters and therefore great opportunity to ask them to promote your event

Ticket bundles – combining a ticket to your event with another offer you have, including showing the value so it is clear how much extra you are providing

Online promotion - as well as your pages, think of relevant groups, whether on LinkedIn or Facebook. If there are a great way to contact your target audience who might be interested in your event. For example, create new event page on LinkedIn to give people the opportunity to post questions and for attendees to network with each other

Other people's audiences – offer to do free training into a relevant group, with the ability to promote your event

External support - this can be in the form of sponsors of the event or other speakers if you choose to go down that route. They will m to promote the event through their marketing channels, to reach their audience

VIP option - opportunity to offer enhanced benefits for a higher price. This also has the FOMO factor

When it comes to event promotion, having a solid marketing strategy in place is the number one priority. But the best marketing plan in the world will not help if the event is not the best it can be. Making it specific to your target audience means they are most likely to rave about it, especially to other like-minded people.

And putting as much energy into marketing to your attendees' pre-event will make for a greater level of success on the day.

Pre event network group - set up an online group that attendees can join once they have bought a ticket to your event. This is a great way to create buzz about joining, . And and your opportunity to provide value information and connection opportunities beforehand. This will help get the word out about your event because they'll talk to other people about it. Word of mouth is a great way to market your event

Attendee Marketing - when someone registers, give them different ways to share the news that they're joining you. For example, this could be social media links to templates they can use and share. And you have the ability to incentivise them to send the booking link to other people they know will be interested. I would suggest you offer them a promotion or a bonus for sharing

Build a dedicated sales page - this will be an early interaction for people who are interested in your event. Make sure it's easy to navigate and provide all the relevant information to convince them to book a ticket. Ideally, if you run a previous event, include a video or at least images from that to help you bring it to life for the person on the page. As importantly, reinforce the benefit of them joining the event. And it goes without saying that you to have a simple booking system

Update on ticket sales - provide regular updates on the number of tickets already gone and the number left. This will encourage people who are waiting till the last minute that if they do, they'll miss out. A bit like the famous retailer whose line is 'once it's gone, it's gone'. It helps focus their mind on 'book tickets now'

Bring a Friend - to encourage early ticket takers to recommend a friend, with an incentive linked

Sales platforms - as well as your dedicated sales page, you have options to use include on event booking pages such as Eventbrite. The positive is getting you in front of a wider audience, but the negative is you will Pay Commission on any ticket sold on their platform. So it is your decision to decide on the cost/benefit of doing this

Ambassadors and Volunteers - a great opportunity to recruit people to help you sell out your event. You could provide them a complementary event ticket or a VIP ticket. Or maybe branded merchandise that only they would have. Plus additional incentives if they promote your event

Sponsorship - you have the ability to charge other people or organisations to be a headline sponsor or part of a sponsor group through to sponsoring an after- party. In return, they have opportunities to promote their business, both before and on the day (for example, sponsoring a table). You could also extend this to goody bags by charging a fee to be part of it.

For securing sponsors, think about how you want to do it. For example, you have an opportunity to promote this option to your own audience. Where you provide key details about how many are attending, the reach of your event, and reasons as to why they should sponsor. And you can include their ability to select being a headline sponsor or sponsor by adding it onto the buy ticket page.

Sponsorship is really about returning investment for them and generation of income for you.

After the event, gathering data and feedback is really important. You have a fantastic opportunity to survey the attendees and ask them for feedback on the event. Not only does this make running the next event easier, but also gives you valuable information. Remember post event is about talking about your offer but also, if appropriate, what your down- sell offer is. So the more you know about your audience, the more successful you're going to be doing this.

This is explored in more detail in 'Podium Profits' in the next chapter.

In summary
Point A: Fear of failing to sell out a single event and getting silence when you try to fill them
Point B: consistently selling out events through proven processes and crushing your targets

Chapter 10: Podium Profits

Speaking on stage is a way to position yourself as a thought leader and authority in your market. You have the ability to showcase your experience and perspective, plus the undivided attention of the people in front of you. And a great opportunity to sell from that stage. But you don't want to come across as a sleazy salesperson.

This is all about how to develop irresistible offers and monetise your message without being a sleazy sales person.

The 3 learning outcomes are

1. How to develop compelling and irresistible offers to maximise conversion rates. By knowing what it is that your target customer wants today

2. How to close sales in the room by using offer strategies that directly appeal to your audience. So they'd climb mountains to have it

3. How to confidently promote your offer to your audience who cannot wait to buy. By knowing that you've practiced, practiced, practiced and now you have something amazing to offer

To be able to have the confidence to stand on a stage is one thing. But your ability to sell is what makes it worthwhile in terms of leveraging it to grow your business.

But knowing how to confidently sell may not be a natural attribute. And there is a very big difference between speaking so that you educate, entertain and motivate your audience versus using speaking to be able to sell your offer. With the game changer being is your ability to give your audience a real reason to take action, ideally in the room.

And although you know this would be great for your business, you might still be holding yourself back for the following reasons

1. Worried that your offer doesn't address what your audience wants. But instead of worrying, why not do the research it takes to ensure that what it is you're going to talk about is absolutely what your target customer wants. And more importantly, wants today

2. Fear that your audience will switch off when you start talking about the offer that you've got for them. And in a direct selling approach this may well happen. Which is why indirect selling where you plant the seeds throughout your talk, and ask their permission to talk about your offer, is a much more effective approach.

For example in direct selling, "I'm sharing fantastic stuff with you today but I only have x time with you. For you to really benefit from (signature offer) you are going to want to (do x eg join, buy, download). I will give you how you can do this at the end".

Vs indirect selling, "I love the framework I'm sharing with you today. Every time I take people through this, it's super powerful. I'm there with and able to walk you through it step by step. Everyone leaves the room hasn't having been able to do (x the outcome)".

3, Dread that no one shows any interest on the day. This is unlikely to happen if you follow the structured approach that I've suggested. However, in that unlikely event your plan will still include following up the members of your audience. Both in terms of your offer, but also if they're not ready to be able to talk about a down- sell offer

In order to have a structured and well-practiced approach, the first step is to do research on your audience in detail long before the actual event. It is an essential step because the more you know about the people in the room, the better you can tailor your presentation and offer. Your objective? To engage those people from the first second you step onto that stage.

Before you commit to speaking, whether that's developing your own event or on somebody else's stage, you need to make sure that the audience is full of your target customer. You'll give a great talk, but not achieve the tangible outcome that you want. As in more customers and more sales.

In Sold Out Success System, I include about how important the title is to your event. Here I go further

You want to link your event subject and offer - essentially the event is a build up to you pitching your offer. Where throughout the event you're giving your target customer a taste of what you do and what the outcome could be for them. You're going to give them loads of value throughout the event. And your offer is your ability to show them, then get even more value from you.

Think about if your event and your offer are not connected. They will feel like a disconnect with everybody in the room.

And your offer is less likely to be bought.

You have already gone through Storytelling Sorcerer and Stage Presence Mastery so I'm not going to go over that ground again.

In summary, it is about telling stories, making it personal, building suspense, showing them, not telling them, and ending with something that's really memorable. For example, a take- away or call to action that's a memorable thing and not easily forgotten. And overall, it's creating an emotional connection because your audience is much more likely to remember how you made them feel than the actual content of the talk.

There are a variety of ways to weave soft selling techniques into your talk

Asking permission - you have the option right at the beginning to ask your audience if you mind sharing about your offer at the end. For example, early on you can explain the absolute amazing value that you're going to provide throughout the time that you're talking to your audience. And then simply ask, ' if I deliver the level of value that I've promised you, would you be OK at the end if I talk to you about how you gain even more value?'. The response is likely to be a positive one

Day event - if you have a day with your audience, it is more than acceptable to pitch before the lunch break as well as at the end. Linked to the above explain that to them up front. Being this transparent with your audience is much more likely to get their buy in on commitment

Extra bonuses - if you want to incentivize your potential customer to buy on the day, offering additional bonuses only available on that day is a great incentive for those people who are thinking about it

Breaks - you can offer the opportunity to have a chat with you about how they could get even more value from you during the break. This is especially relevant if you have a lunch break because you can have time slots that they can book on to. And you could use WhatsApp, QR code etc to make it easy

Commitment - for anyone who is seriously thinking about buying but not on the day, you give them the option to book time with you post event. And as part of the information that you give them, you can provide the detail around your offer

Next, is placing small calls to action throughout your talk. Planting little seeds as you include features of your offer. This is not direct selling where you are transparent about letting your audience know this is your offer. To be transparent, at the beginning you might say that you're going to share lots of information about your offer to get their interest straight away.

What I am recommending for you is indirect selling as it's more subtle. Because it's about building your audience up to get curious about what's coming next. For example, you could casually say that this is something you share in your chats with customers or your book or your course, etc. Drawing additional attention to your specific offer.

This means that by the time you get to the final part of your talk, your audience have already heard snippets about your offer a few times. And hopefully they've become interested in learning more about it.

Then you can say something like, "now, you've heard me talk about my (what your signature approach is called), which I have referred to while I have been talking to you today. So if ok with you, I would like to (your call to action – whether an offer to buy or a next step)".

You could even get agreement from the room like you did at the beginning by instead saying something like, "now we are in the final section, would you like to hear a little bit about my (your call to action – whether an offer to buy or a next step)".

Where if you have been seeding through your talk and have entertained and inspired your audience, they will want to hear more about being in your world more.

As part of your story, you can identify challenges that your target customer will resonate with. It gives them a sense that you understand where they're coming from, what it is that they want. You're almost taking them on a road map all the way through to the end where you present your offer.

Give me a reason to want to learn more. For example, share obstacles that you've overcome that they will identify with. You ideally want them to be nodding along with you because they get it and have been there or appreciate what you went through. It all helps to build the trust factor.

Now you've built the foundation to be able to talk more about the action you'd like them to take but in a non-sleazy way. This is more about painting a picture of the outcome for them of taking the action because you know what it is that they would ideally like to do. You will have shown them you understand their struggles and desires and are in a position to be able to help them achieve the positive outcome they deserve.

As you get towards the end of your talk, this is your opportunity to signpost them on action to take. This could be as simple as an offer to answer any questions that they have. Or details of how they can access more information either in the room or on a website. And you can further support their decision to buy by offering them something special on the day. It can be me in the form of an extra bonus, a special price, or special entry to something else as well.

This is about explaining the positive impact. Of accessing your offer. In essence, offering them something that's too good to refuse.

The best marketeers are those that are able to influence people to take action based on something that is a has a positive result for them. Is not about beating people into submission pointing out the disaster that might happen if they don't buy.

This is about a win-win situation. Win for them because they benefit from the outcome that you're offering, and a win for you because you gain a new customer that fits your target.

And this is how you monetise your message be able to sell from any stage. And remember, this is about your chosen customer. It is not about being pushy or sleazy. Or even worse, forgetting to even offer the opportunity for your audience to take the next step with you. Because this is about drawing people in by building the connection.

196

Remember, if you invest great time and energy into your audience and deliver something that's of real value to them, they will be fully engaged and therefore a great time to make your offer.

It may help to remember that you don't have to close everybody in the room. The fact that you've been brave and and courageous enough to stand on a stage is amazing in itself. So you deserve to take pressure off yourself by realizing how many of your widgets you would ideally like to sell that day. And realise it's likely to only be a few. And that is more than doable.

You don't have to show everybody in the room that they need to buy your offer because essentially you only want your target customer to take up your offer.

As to the offer itself, make sure that it naturally inspires a yes. Which seems a great time to talk about crafting and irresistible offer.

The elements you need are

1. A solution your target customer wants today. You need to offer them something they already want or desire. Because convincing someone that they need what you're offering is a very difficult mountain to climb

2. Identify what makes your offer special. What is it about how you do what you do that is so different? Think about how Apple have spent so much time and investment on

design and innovation, means they stand out and their customers feel part of that creativity. Or through developing your own methodology such as the Be In Demand methodology. Where I have developed a signature system based on the 25 years working with big brands on growing their customers and sales and on the last five working with female entrepreneurs to successfully grow theirs

3. Value pricing where you focus on the outcome you create instead the number of hours you might spend doing it. This might seem strange to hear, but if you don't charge enough, it can put potential customers off. Because they perceive you're too cheap! And is interestingly, if the price is more than your customers feel they're getting a better-quality service

4. Make it an easy decision. By packing high perceived value into your offer, helps to make yes an easier decision. This is naturally done through the inclusion of bonuses that have a high perceived value. Adding a price to those bonuses and then adding up all of those costs demonstrates to your potential customer that for what they're paying, they're getting maybe 5 or 10 times the value. You can further support this by offering a guarantee. For example, a money back guarantee there is time based

5. Time. Link to making it an easy decision, you can add extra bonuses based on the making a quick decision

Remember, this is about creating an irresistible offer that your target customer already wants. And by making their decision easier, they are more likely to say yes. But it has to be something they already want.

For example, if I were to offer an audience the ability to buy an umbrella, even though it's a fantastic umbrella, they may not take me up on the offer. However, if I point out that it's torrential rain outside and they are going to get soaked if they don't have an umbrella with them, which most of them don't. Then guess what happens? I am likely to make sales.

You might also want to consider the people in the room who are either not in a position to buy today or want more time to consider that you offer them an alternative. This could be as simple as access to something for free, whether it's a workshop, a download, etc, so that you're able to serve everybody in the room.

It also opens up another opportunity to offer a VIP version which you could charge for. This means that anybody in your audience who's more committed and engaged will self-select that VIP version. For example, linked to the free thing that you're offering, you could attach a private 1-1 with you. People who want to get there faster or who want it's specifically tailored to them.

Also think about what they walk away with. There may be attendees who are interested in buying from you but not on the day. Your ability to follow up with them is

199

important. Consider what elements you provide in the goodie bag as promotion, links you give them access to for more information and physical material eg booklets explaining details.

Well there you go, how to use a stages to sell. And to help you, there is a 'How to Sell Successfully' Checklist.

Now you are set to talk on your own as well as someone else's stage. To help you even further, there is a story framework to use in the next chapter, based on what the movie makers used to use and still do to this day. It is well worn and proven to be a seat filler.

In summary
Point A: feeling invisible, as if you're talking to ghosts with no ears or wallets
Point B: Feeling invincible, having people whip out their credit cards begging to work with you

Chapter 11: The Story Behind My Why

Writing this book was not part of my plan. It happened because after growing my own successful business over five years, I realised I had done it by just being me. No extrovert suit necessary, this is the one I used in my corporate career for over 25 years.

The suit that allowed me to walk into meeting rooms of strangers and hold their attention through to the many stages I had to speak on, where I received positive feedback.

And even though I was transparent in how much anxiety I suffered through doing it, it made no difference, as I was just expected to do it.

Especially as I became more senior where it became an even bigger part of my role as Marketing Director, then Sales and Marketing Director and finally as Managing Director of Consumer Finance. You would think after so many years, I would have grown used to it, especially standing on major stages. But it was never the case. Each time I would have panic attacks, struggle with nerves and physically shake.

The extrovert suit was my saving grace. I managed to put it on every time and deliver. Although I have shared my first experience of professionally speaking in front of very senior people in the first bank I worked for. And how each of us (all management trainees) were torn apart based on our performance.

Now looking back, where we all that awful or was it there way of 'toughening us up'. I will never know for sure.

When I set up my own business, I wanted it to be in person from day one, where I was in the room with my clients, whether individually or in groups. I love the energy of the room and you get so much more accomplished.

It was a way for me to stand out too as everyone else was pretty much purely online.

Getting in front of my target audience was the objective, offering them something they already wanted.

Fast forward five years and I still only work in person. I have made a success of speaking in small groups, running my own events and speaking on other people's stages.

Ah back to the why behind this book.

Using these techniques has been hugely beneficial for my business which is why I want the same for you.

But I also know how challenging it is and to be transparent, I still get nervous today, but not at the high levels of my corporate career. For one simple reason, I now choose to do it.

Which is why if I can inspire just one other person to have the courage to speak in front of their target customer, it is worth spending the time writing this book.

204

I have developed nine steps for you to choose how far you want to step out of your comfort zone. It is your decision whether you want to be more confident speaking in small groups or maybe to test out running your own small event. And maybe then considering speaking on other people's stages.

It is amazing the impact doing this has on your business.

What do you have to lose?

Because you know what, even if you decide it is not for you, at least you have given it a go.

I want to help you because I know how it feels not to be the loudest person in the room. To get lost amongst all the big voices and think 'why am I here?'.

Just between us, the loudest in the room is not necessarily the most successful either. I have found this out more than once.

Why can't you be one of the women who is quietly successful? Getting on with building relationships and deep connections which result in your business growing even more.

Please come and join me in being in front of your target customers. It is a whole load more fun than thinking 'what can my next reel be about' or 'why am I spending so much time on doing a post when only a few people see it'.

205

Time to increase your impact by celebrating who you are and showing those who you want to buy from you, how amazing that would be for them!!!

Chapter 12: Story Framework

Your story connects you to your customers on a deeper level.

Businesses, big and small, who share their story are much more likely to be successful because telling stories helps drive sales. So a well told story can really make a difference in securing a sale or not because it demonstrates you have a purpose so is important in your messaging. Purpose shows prospective customers you are passionate about solving their issues or supporting them in their desires.

The world is so noisy today, especially online so it is easy to get lost in all that. Story telling as part of your message distinguishes you from your competition.

Telling your story is one of the most powerful marketing tools you have. Think back to yesterday, how many stories did you tell? 'Strange question and none' you might answer.

But I guarantee if you spoke to someone, you told a story. Could have been if you met up, how you got there or a problem you are having at the moment or something you are celebrating.

You will have used a story to explain your point and it is something we do without even being aware of it.

Well until I have now pointed it out to you!!!

Why Do We Like Stories So Much?

We are hardwired to love stories from being children. If you have children, nieces, nephews or think back to when you were young. Stories are devoured by children and if any of them are like my 5 year old nephew, once I have read him a story, guess what he says next? 'Again'. And the process repeats. Or the last time you met a friend and shared what was going on in your lives. All story based.

Consider way back to cavemen and Ancient Egyptians, they told stories through pictures on walls.

And coming back to today, consider the phenomenal growth of reality TV. We cannot get enough of 'normal' people and their lives. Let alone how successful soap operas are.

Ah hopefully you are getting the picture – stories are all around us.

Telling Your Story

Just in the same way Wonder Woman has an origin story, so do you. There is a reason you set up your business and why you are where you are today. And prospective and existing customers would be interested in it as it means they get to know you a little more, to support this and use a cliché 'people buy from people'.

For example, my own is as an accidental entrepreneur because I never dreamed of having my own business. I loved my corporate career for over 25 years and was passionate about working with big brand, fantastic marketing agencies and developing phenomenal teams.

That is until the day I no longer did and decided to walk away. I wanted to find a new passion and set about learning lots of new skills, including qualifying as a teacher, mentor, coach and half a counsellor as well as diplomas in sugarcraft, floristry and natural skincare formulation.

But it took a lady whose craft workshop I was on to have fresh eyes. As I was helping her with ideas for marketing her small business, she simply said 'why don't you do this for a living'. DOH!!! So that afternoon, I set up my own business.

Who knew I would end up working with the most amazing female entrepreneurs who I have the pleasure of being able to help, to make a real difference and impact on the growth of their businesses.

I can share the obstacles I had along the way, for example, my brother called me every week for the first 12 months, with the same question 'got a proper job yet?'.

Ah the phone rang again, I saw the number and just knew what my brother would say. Sure enough, picked up the phone, 'have you got a proper job yet?' And every week for my first 12 months just like groundhog day, my heart would drop as the feeling of dread would fill my head, because I knew what my brother would say.

No 'how are you?' or 'how is it going', just whether I had come to my senses and gone back to work for someone else.

How many times have you heard a similar line from well-meaning family and friends? Do you ever feel like it is too much, even though you have spent so much time and effort?

Who knew having your own business could be so tough? And then the seed of doubt gets amplified when a member of your own family or a friend breathes life into that niggling doubt.

So groundhog happened every week for 52 weeks but I did not let it stop me. Just because my brother wanted the warm comfort of a guaranteed monthly salary, working for someone else, it was not my passion any more.

Once Upon a Time Process

In the examples shared, I have included a start, middle and an end, just like all good stories.

It is a standard approach and if you want to go next level, that is where the Hollywood movie process comes in (and all great Disney movies).

There is a set formula. It is called the Hero's Journey and is told in three parts.

Part 1 often referred to as Departure

Covering who it is all about (the hero), where they are, what their problems are and where they are going. The premise is they get called to take on an adventure (for example, to start a new business) but something stops them, until they meet someone who convinces them to continue on.

Part 2 often referred to as Initiation

This is where the hero experiences some successes and failures (think in terms of a rollercoaster in terms of dropping down but then finding a way to come back up). Where they experience different tests along the way and have to overcome hurdles.

Part 3 often referred to as the Return

Where the hero hits their lowest point, but more importantly how they cope and finds their way through. After experiencing the failures, they find solutions, achieve success and end triumphant.

Recognise any movies now. Blockbuster origin stories follow this formula, consider Star Wars for example, where Luke's objective is to save Princess Leia and restore the Republic back to its glory.

Or Raiders of the Lost Ark where Indiana Jones is willing to risk everything to find the Ark before the baddies do, to stop them being invincible and take over the world,

Now I appreciate your story may not be so dramatic but the key elements are still there.

Part 1 often referred to as Departure

Why you started your own business, what your why is. What obstacles were in your way initially and who helped you.

Part 2 often referred to as Initiation

In any business, you experience successes and failures along the way. But you continued on even though they tested your resolve.

Part 3 often referred to as the Return

Even at your lowest point, you still found a way through, to be where you are today. You have experienced so much already but you continue on as you remember your 'why' of doing this.

Pen and paper ready...once upon a time...

Chapter 13: The Author

Hi I am Lisa, from corporate marketing to a successful accidental entrepreneur.

An award winner, author and international speaker, with proven results as a successful In-Person Growth Mentor, working locally in the West Midlands and Worcestershire.

I champion female entrepreneurs as for far too long, too many remain in the shadows and hidden, so I want you to step out and make the impact you deserve.

It is why I show extraordinary female entrepreneurs how to stand out and create demand for what you do, through my signature Be In Demand Methodology, where customers approach you to buy and you grow the business you dream of.

And with over 25 years' big brand experience including Selfridges, Asda, Marriott, Peugeot and Harvey Nichols, I use the same proven processes, tools and techniques to build and grow my own successful small business and is what I share with my customers to grow theirs.

My mission each year is to work face to face with 1000 local female entrepreneurs to show you how to up level your marketing and be fiercely in demand.

I work with extraordinary female entrepreneurs who are ready to stand out, as I show you how to create demand for what you do, so customers approach you and you grow the business you dream of.

Best decision I ever made was walking away from my successful corporate career, after over 25 years building an extensive portfolio of marketing skills, because now I get to use all the stuff I learned and get to choose who I work with. It is how I became an accidental entrepreneur so I now get to wake up happy and do what I love to do every day.

Set up with no any start up investment or experience of running a small business, just an idea. To identify what makes you special and build marketing strategies that are easy to do and you are comfortable with. And what gives me great pleasure as I can make a difference to someone else's life and have freedom of time.

But it has been a tough road and one I sometimes thought of leaving but I am so glad I stuck at it.
And even my own family were doubters. I still vividly remember how the phone rang every week and my heart sank as I saw who was calling because it was Groundhog Day again. 'Got a job yet?' The same opening line that I heard each time even though I had my own business.

I am so grateful for the support I received and continue to receive from my fabulous business buddies, who like me have never given up no matter what family or friends ever said. And I wake up happy and do what I love to do every day

Three mantras from my Grandad, who is still my hero, remain core to my life. 1. Every day is a gift where you can

218

be kind to other, 2. Laugh until it hurts. And 3. Do what you love to do. Thanks Grandad!!!

I love having Random Tuesdays, when with my best pal, we learn random new skills like silver clay jewellery and glass fusion! I love that my nieces and nephews, who are young adults now, chose to spend time with me because they want to and I love a treatment where you get to drift away to the plinky plonky music (actual term, who knew that!) and all those really gorgeous and luxury aromas.

Being able to successfully grow the business I dream of means I can help so many, including continuing to run free marketing workshops, donating my marketing skills to a charity every year and having the time to be able to speak to groups of incredible female entrepreneurs to champion them as I share ways to level up their marketing.

Worst decision going platinum blonde and being able to pull out big clumps of my hair, luckily I have thick hair.

I have qualifications and the certificates to prove it, in natural skincare formulator, floristry, sugar craft, aromatherapy, professional gift wrapping and modern lettering, for no other reason than it is fun to learn.

Oh and BONUS celebrity info of first most bizarre moment standing in the queue to the loos at The Brit awards (which I had the opportunity to go to every year through my job), with Katie Price on one side and Scissor Sisters on the other. Second enjoying the champagne and cream tea at

219

Wimbledon so much we missed all the matches, including seats that were next to the players families. And third having lunch next to David Schwimmer and Michael Parkinson (two separate occasions) but not realising until we left the restaurant (being observant is not a superpower).

My final thought is that life is so much more fun when you take risks as who knows what will happen!

WHO KNEW I would be an accidental entrepreneur. Which still makes me smile to think back to all those times in reviews, when I was asked what my 5-year plan was in my corporate days. I would say I wanted to be an international woman of mystery. Or have my own marketing agency, where I worked with the best creatives and cherry picked the clients we worked with.

Guess what, I am living my dream.

I am grateful each and every day for that. And even on those days which are really tough and nothing seems to be going the way I want them too, I never think 'oh I wish I was back there'. Because this is exactly where I am supposed to be.

And guess what...

I still treat every day as a gift. Laugh until it hurts. And I wake up happy and get to do what you love to do every day. Winner, winner, chicken dinner, wonderful ladies. And thanks again Grandad.

It would be a pleasure to have you within my virtual world.

You can find me here

http://beindemand.uk
Facebook.com/beindemand.uk
Instagram.com/beindemand
Linkedin.com/lisasimcox

Thank you for reading xx

Chapter 14: Resources

In each of the nine steps of my Pavement to Podium framework, I have talked about the supporting resource available to you.

It is easy to access them all, by going onto my website

http://beindemand.uk/pavement-to-podium.

You will find all the details of how to access the free resources.

Chapter 15: Final Thoughts

What would you say if you were asked 'why do you love what you do'.

For me it is simple, having impact. Making a real difference to other women's businesses but importantly their confidence and positive effect on their lives.

It is a pleasure to be able to do what I do. And I am so grateful to the ladies who trust me. I now have my dream business where I chose who I work with, I choose when I work and I choose who I spend time with.

I am thankful every day to be where I am. Which is why I want to give 'choice' to anyone I work directly with. But also in my wider world of influence too.

I work with amazing women who are super passionate about what they do. Being able to share my knowledge, experience and expertise from a toolbox built over 30 years is fantastically rewarding. Seeing the ripple effect is incredible too.

As I watch those powerful women support, inspire and cheerlead each other. What truly lights my fire is seeing the impact.

Having my own successful small business gives the ability to mentor other local small business owners to do the same. Local because I only work face to face. Where the energy in the room is so much stronger and helps me be more effective as I can gauge reactions and comfort levels. And importantly make sure no one is left behind.

My corporate career was my training ground to what I do today. Who knew working for over 25 years with those big brands would enable me to show other women how to achieve the income and impact they deserve. Plus a further 5 in growing a small business where I have choice.

A lot of that success has been through getting in front of my target customer, which is what I have shared in this book.

I have said it a few times, about it being scary when you are not one of the loudest in the room. But if you can find ways to go into those rooms, wow the results are amazing.

My final thought for you is, what do you have to lose?

Printed in Great Britain
by Amazon

48335964R00129